Nmap Essentials

Harness the power of Nmap, the most versatile
network port scanner on the planet, to secure
large scale networks

David Shaw

BIRMINGHAM - MUMBAI

Nmap Essentials

First published: May 2015

Production reference: 1220515

Published by Packt Publishing Ltd.
Livery Place
35 Livery Street
Birmingham B3 2PB, UK.

ISBN 978-1-78355-406-5

www.packtpub.com

Credits

Author
David Shaw

Reviewers
Rajdeep Bhattacharya

Nikhil Kumar

Aravinda Babu T

Ravi Chandra Vinjanampati

Commissioning Editor
Amarabha Banerjee

Acquisition Editor
Shaon Basu

Content Development Editor
Siddhesh Salvi

Technical Editor
Madhunikita Sunil Chindarkar

Copy Editor
Trishya Hajare

Project Coordinator
Nidhi Joshi

Proofreaders
Stephen Copestake

Safis Editing

Indexer
Hemangini Bari

Production Coordinator
Nitesh Thakur

Cover Work
Nitesh Thakur

About the Author

David Shaw has extensive experience in many areas of information security. He began working in the trenches of perimeter analysis and conducting external threat research for large financial institutions. After switching to offensive security, he joined Redspin to conduct application security assessments and network penetration tests.

David is currently the Chief Technology Officer and Vice President of Professional Services at Redspin, specializing in external and application security, and managing a team of highly skilled engineers. He has particular interests in complex threat modeling and unconventional attack vectors, and has been a speaker at THOTCON, NolaCon, ToorCon, LayerOne, DEF CON, BSides Las Vegas, BSides Los Angeles, and BSides Seattle.

About the Reviewers

Rajdeep Bhattacharya is a Principal Server Engineer at Nimbuzz Technologies, located in Gurgaon, India. He has been working on the security and scalability of different products for Nimbuzz. Currently, he is working on the behavior-driven development approach and the performance optimization of various caching layers. In his spare time, he enjoys listening to music, travelling, cooking, and playing table tennis.

Nikhil Kumar is an Information Security Analyst at Biz2Credit Inc. He is a Certified Ethical Hacker, and has a bachelor's and master's degree in computer science. He has written many articles on web application security, security coding practices, web application firewalls, and so on.

He has discovered multiple vulnerabilities in big hotshot applications, including Apple, Microsoft, and so on.

He is currently pursuing the OSCP certification.

Nikhil can be contacted on LinkedIn at `https://in.linkedin.com/in/nikhil73`.

I would like to thank my family for their support. I would also like to thank my friends, mentor Jatin Jain, and Swati Bhardwaj who helped me in every situation. Next, I would like to thank everybody at Packt Publishing for giving me this opportunity.

Aravinda Babu T is a senior staff member at Fornetix. In this role, he focuses on architecture and the development of encryption key orchestration technologies. He previously worked as an advisory software engineer in IBM Software Labs for the power servers division, and as an open source contributor in ONF for the wireless and mobility group. He has 14 years of experience in network security, datacom, and mobile technologies. He has also worked at Nokia, Motorola, and IBM previously. His experience includes mobile middleware, wireless LAN switches, UTM appliances, and HPC servers.

Ravi Chandra Vinjanampati has been working in the infosec domain for the past 7 years. He holds a GCIH certification, has worked with global finance giants in the past, and is currently working with an engineering company.

www.PacktPub.com

Support files, eBooks, discount offers, and more

For support files and downloads related to your book, please visit
www.PacktPub.com.

Did you know that Packt offers eBook versions of every book published,
with PDF and ePub files available? You can upgrade to the eBook version at
www.PacktPub.com and as a print book customer, you are entitled to a discount on
the eBook copy. Get in touch with us at service@packtpub.com for more details.

At www.PacktPub.com, you can also read a collection of free technical articles,
sign up for a range of free newsletters and receive exclusive discounts and offers
on Packt books and eBooks.

https://www2.packtpub.com/books/subscription/packtlib

Do you need instant solutions to your IT questions? PacktLib is Packt's online digital
book library. Here, you can search, access, and read Packt's entire library of books.

Why subscribe?

- Fully searchable across every book published by Packt
- Copy and paste, print, and bookmark content
- On demand and accessible via a web browser

Free access for Packt account holders

If you have an account with Packt at www.PacktPub.com, you can use this to access
PacktLib today and view 9 entirely free books. Simply use your login credentials for
immediate access.

Table of Contents

Preface

This book is designed to teach readers how to run Nmap, one of the most powerful network security tools ever created. I'm excited to walk you through learning this tool, as well as the various different elements that come with it—for example, the Nmap Scripting Engine and other tools like Ncat and Ncrack. Throughout this book, we'll be walking through techniques, tips, and tricks to help you learn the essentials of Nmap in a fast and efficient manner!

What this book covers

Chapter 1, *Introduction to Nmap*, reviews the history of Nmap, what the tool does, when it will be used, how the product evolved, and how to install Nmap on Windows, Linux, and OS X.

Chapter 2, *Network Fundamentals*, is about how networks work and why a port scanner is important. It overviews TCP, UDP, port scanning, common ports, and service banners.

Chapter 3, *Nmap Basics*, covers how to run basic or normal Nmap scans without complex flags.

Chapter 4, *Advanced Nmap Scans*, is about the advanced flags in Nmap that can designate different types of scans.

Chapter 5, *Performance Optimization*, is about how to optimize timing, parallelism, and so on, in Nmap in order to complete scans efficiently.

Chapter 6, *Introduction to the Nmap Scripting Engine*, is about the Nmap scripting engine—what it is, how it works, what programming language it uses, and popular Nmap scripts to use.

Chapter 7, *Writing Nmap Scripts*, teaches the reader how to create a basic Nmap script in Lua.

Chapter 8, *Additional Nmap Tools*, covers the other tools that come with the Nmap suite—Nrack, Nping, and Ncat.

Chapter 9, *Vulnerability Assessments and Tools*, explains the relationships between Nmap and other tools commonly used in professional vulnerability assessments.

Chapter 10, *Penetration Testing with Metasploit*, is about the interaction of Nmap with penetration testing tools such as Metasploit.

What you need for this book

In order to follow along with this book, you need to have a working computer running either Windows, Linux, or Mac OS X. We'll be installing Nmap and VirtualBox as part of running through this book; these are two free pieces of software that can help us run network scans. Additionally, an Internet or local network connection is valuable for trying out scans.

Who this book is for

This book is aimed at beginners who have experience as a system administrator or of network engineering, and wish to get started with Nmap. Advanced users can use this book as a reference, or to understand when certain key aspects of the software should be used.

The style and approach of this book is like an easy-to-follow guide full of real-world examples that demonstrate how and when to use different aspects of the Nmap suite. Clear and concise writing makes this introductory-level book an ideal guide to start with. Each topic covers examples from the real world, enabling the reader to easily progress from an Nmap beginner to an advanced user.

Conventions

In this book, you will find a number of text styles that distinguish between different kinds of information. Here are some examples of these styles, and an explanation of their meaning.

Code words in text, database table names, folder names, filenames, file extensions, pathnames, dummy URLs, user input, and Twitter handles are shown as follows: "If you want to make Nmap less verbose than normal, you can also use the `--reduce-verbosity` flag."

A block of code is set as follows:

```
action = function(host, port)
local robots = http.get(host, port, "/robots.txt")

if robots.status == 200 then
  return "robots.txt status 200"
else
  return "robots.txt status: " .. robots.status
end
end
```

New terms and **important words** are shown in bold. Words that you see on the screen, for example, in menus or dialog boxes, appear in the text like this: "Once the scan is completed, clicking on **Vulnerabilities** shows the current list of vulnerabilities detected on the target scope."

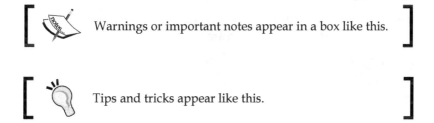

Warnings or important notes appear in a box like this.

Tips and tricks appear like this.

Reader feedback

Feedback from our readers is always welcome. Let us know what you think about this book—what you liked or disliked. Reader feedback is important for us as it helps us develop titles that you will really get the most out of.

To send us general feedback, simply e-mail feedback@packtpub.com, and mention the book's title in the subject of your message.

If there is a topic that you have expertise in and you are interested in either writing or contributing to a book, see our author guide at www.packtpub.com/authors.

Customer support

Now that you are the proud owner of a Packt book, we have a number of things to help you to get the most from your purchase.

Downloading the example code

You can download the example code files from your account at `http://www.packtpub.com` for all the Packt Publishing books you have purchased. If you purchased this book elsewhere, you can visit `http://www.packtpub.com/support` and register to have the files e-mailed directly to you.

Errata

Although we have taken every care to ensure the accuracy of our content, mistakes do happen. If you find a mistake in one of our books—maybe a mistake in the text or the code—we would be grateful if you could report this to us. By doing so, you can save other readers from frustration and help us improve subsequent versions of this book. If you find any errata, please report them by visiting `http://www.packtpub.com/submit-errata`, selecting your book, clicking on the **Errata Submission Form** link, and entering the details of your errata. Once your errata are verified, your submission will be accepted and the errata will be uploaded to our website, or added to any list of existing errata, under the Errata section of that title.

To view the previously submitted errata, go to `https://www.packtpub.com/books/content/support` and enter the name of the book in the search field. The required information will appear under the **Errata** section.

Piracy

Piracy of copyrighted material on the Internet is an ongoing problem across all media. At Packt, we take the protection of our copyright and licenses very seriously. If you come across any illegal copies of our works, in any form, on the Internet, please provide us with the location address or website name immediately so that we can pursue a remedy.

Please contact us at `copyright@packtpub.com` with a link to the suspected pirated material.

We appreciate your help in protecting our authors, and our ability to bring you valuable content.

Questions

If you have a problem with any aspect of this book, you can contact us at
questions@packtpub.com, and we will do our best to address the problem.

1
Introduction to Nmap

Before we get started with the technical intricacies of mastering Nmap, it's a good idea to understand how Nmap itself began and evolved as a project. This tool has been around for almost twenty years, and is a well-loved and often-used component across many technical industries.

In this chapter, we will cover:

- How the Nmap project began
- The evolution of the tool itself
- New add-ons to the Nmap suite
- How to install Nmap on Windows, OS X, and Linux

Nmap's humble beginnings

Nmap started from humble beginnings. Unlike the commercial security tools that are released today, the very first Nmap was only about 2,000 lines of code—and was released in 1997 in issue 51 of Phrack, a hacker "zine" that was started in 1985. Nmap's timeline is a fascinating one, and its growth has been phenomenal. The general timeline of Nmap development is as follows:

- At the time of release, Nmap did not have very many features; in fact, it was bare bones. There was no version number attached to this release of Nmap because the developers did not plan to release any future versions. Nmap was designed only to scan for open ports on a target machine, and only worked when run from a Linux host and compiled with gcc.

- Only four days after the initial release of Nmap, though, a slightly improved version was released (also through Phrack) — version 1.25. It was becoming very clear, even in the infancy of the now-famous tool, that there was an extremely high demand for a high-performance port scanner. Although there had previously been ways to detect open ports, Nmap made it straightforward to assess a third-party host over the Internet or across a local network. The hacker community was intrigued.

- By March 1998, about six months after the initial Nmap release, the scanner had become the de facto port scanner of the underground hacker community and blossoming information security industry. Renaud Deraison asked permission to use the scanner code in a new vulnerability assessment engine he was creating, and (after receiving permission) Nmap scanning technology became integrated with the very first version of Nessus.

- By September 2003, when Nmap 3.45 was released, there had been many major changes to the project. Fyodor, the primary developer, is now working on maintaining Nmap full-time. The tool has many new features — such as service detection, OS detection, timing configuration, and optimization flags (all of which will be covered later in this book) — and has truly reached a state of maturity.

- In December 2006, one of the most important aspects of the Nmap project was integrated into all Nmap builds: **Nmap Scripting Engine** (**NSE**). The NSE allows users of Nmap to write their own modules (in a programming language called **Lua**) to trigger on certain ports being open, or certain services — or even specific versions of services — found listening. This release allows the elevation of Nmap from a simple networking tool to a fully robust and customizable vulnerability assessment engine, suitable for a wide variety of tasks.

The many uses of Nmap

Although port scanning is obviously very important for security professionals — after all, without understanding what network ports are open, it would be impossible to assess the security of a system — Nmap is also very valuable for other types of information technology professionals.

System administrators use Nmap to determine which of their systems are online, so they can understand if there are problems or inconsistencies on their network. Similarly, using OS detection and service detection, these administrators are able to easily verify that all systems are running the same (hopefully current) versions of operating systems and network-enabled software.

Because of its ability to change timing, as well as set specific flags on different packets (for example, the **Xmas Tree** scan), developers can turn to Nmap for help in testing embedded network stacks, in order to verify that the aggressive network traffic won't have unintended outcomes that may crash a system.

Lastly — and perhaps most importantly — students of network and computer engineering are major users of Nmap. Because it is a free and open source software, there is no barrier to get the software and run it immediately. Even amateur users scanning their own small home networks can learn an immense amount about how their computers and networks work and are configured by seeing what services are online. Although there are Windows and OS X ports, Nmap is also a great introduction to running straightforward (but advanced) tools on the Linux command line.

Installing Nmap

On most modern operating systems (Windows, OS X, and most distributions of Linux), installing Nmap is a very easy task. The official Nmap website (http://insecure.org/) distributes downloadable installers for Windows and Mac OS X that are very easy to run.

For Windows, a full walk-through of the installation process is available at http://nmap.org/book/inst-windows.html.

For Mac OS X, a full walk-through of the installation process is available at http://nmap.org/book/inst-macosx.html.

To install Nmap for Linux, there are several options. The most recent "**bleeding edge**" builds are always available to install from source (see the following paragraph). There are RPMs that can be downloaded from the http://insecure.org/ website, but most Linux distributions already have Nmap in their standard packages' repositories.

To install from a repository on Debian/Ubuntu is very straightforward. First, run sudo apt-get update to verify that all 'apt sources' lists are up to date. Then, it is as simple as sudo apt-get install Nmap to download and install a working version of Nmap!

Building Nmap from source

To install Nmap from source, three steps must be taken:

1. Download the source code.
2. Compile the code.
3. Install the compiled tool.

Downloading the code with a tool such as wget is very simple; all we need to do is type wget http://nmap.org/dist/nmap-6.47.tar.bz2 (or whatever is the current version of Nmap).

Once the tool is downloaded, it must be removed from its tarball — or compressed — state. This is done using the tar command by typing tar xvf nmap-6.47.tar.bz2.

At this stage, we now have a new directory filled with Nmap source code. If we change the directory by typing cd nmap-6.47, we are then able to compile this code. For those users that are familiar with installing tools on Linux, the next step will be familiar. We need to ./configure make and sudo make install in order to install Nmap on our system.

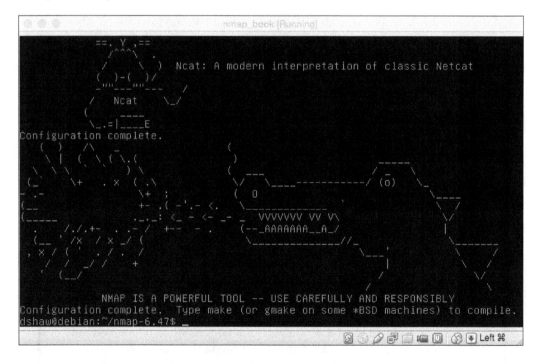

The "Nmap dragon" is a famous piece of ASCII art that is displayed during the
./configure step of Nmap source code compilation.

Once Nmap is successfully installed, you can verify that it works — and see which
options it was compiled with — by typing nmap -V. We'll cover the different flags that
you can pass to Nmap in the subsequent chapters.

```
                              nmap_book (Running)
dshaw@debian:~$ nmap -V

Nmap version 6.47 ( http://nmap.org )
Platform: i686-pc-linux-gnu
Compiled with: nmap-liblua-5.2.3 nmap-libpcre-7.6 nmap-libpcap-1.2.1 nmap-libdne
t-1.12 ipv6
Compiled without: openssl
Available nsock engines: epoll poll select
dshaw@debian:~$ _
```

Summary

After reading this chapter, you should have a solid understanding of the wonderful
background that Nmap brings to the information security world. Starting as a small
project, the Nmap project is now one of the pillars of several industries.

If you have followed the installation instructions, you should now have a fully
functional copy of Nmap ready to work with throughout the rest of the chapters.
If not, now would be a great time to go ahead and install the tool so that you are
ready to start scanning, auditing, and assessing!

In the next chapter, we will learn the basics of TCP/IP networking in order to
better understand how Nmap is able to assess open ports, and find out which
services and operating systems are running.

2
Network Fundamentals

Before it's possible for us to use Nmap as a tool, we first need to understand the very basics of how it works. In order to scan networks (including the Internet), we must initially understand the concepts on which all networks are built. Although this book will not describe in-depth networking concepts — you won't become a *packet ninja* by learning to use Nmap — we do need to ensure that we can interpret the scan results from standard and advanced Nmap scans. Without the fundamentals of networking, we will not be able to scan at all!

The following topics will be covered in this chapter:

- How networks work
- The difference between TCP and UDP
- An introduction to ports
- How port scanning works
- How service version detection and banner grabbing work

The structure of the Internet

Before we go into some of the complexities of networked software, it's important to understand how the Internet itself is designed. In many ways, the Internet functions the same as a large network that you might have at your home or office — the difference, of course, is that instead of workstations, the Internet has Internet-facing services. Most homes, for example, have many computers that are on the same **Local Area Network (LAN)**, but only one IP address on the Internet. If someone were to scan this network from their Internet-connected device, they would only see Internet-facing services — not each family member's individual computer. This is important to note because across the Internet, only ports that are forwarded to a machine may be accessible on a given IP address. There are some exceptions to this rule that we will look at later.

When scanning a computer on your LAN, however, you will generally be able to see all the ports that are open. This is because when packets are traveling on a local network, rather than over the Internet, you have direct access to the target machine — you don't have to pass through a router or switch that would block all of these ports over the Internet. This is why, for example, when hosting a server at a LAN party, no one has to forward any ports in a third-party device.

When conducting scans throughout the rest of this book, please keep in mind that there are several different elements that may help or stop the scan from detecting every service that is listening. We'll go through some of the pitfalls in later chapters, and give useful work-arounds whenever possible.

The OSI model

To understand how packets — which are the bits of information that travel from one machine to another — run networks, it's a good idea to have a basic idea of the **Open Systems Interconnection (OSI)** model. This is a conceptual way to think about how networks work on different layers. It's easy to understand that physically, networks are just pieces of hardware with electrical signals running across them; it's actually much more difficult to conceptualize the logical networks that developers and network operations staff (as well as computers) work with.

The simplest explanation is that different protocols and bits of information work on different layers of the model, and work off of each other. The following diagram briefly explains which layer performs which role, so that we can understand how service banners and ports work later in this chapter.

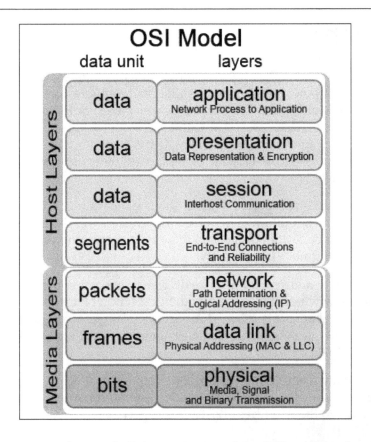

It isn't necessary to understand all the intricacies of the OSI model or low-level networking in order to use Nmap effectively, and to interpret scan results that are accurate. It is necessary, however, to realize that not all networking information is created equally—some information is readily accessible at certain times, while it is more difficult to access certain data at other times. If you're interested in learning more about networking from an in-depth perspective, it's worth checking out tools such as Wireshark that can capture packets or view them in transit.

Port scanning

Nmap is a port scanner, but we haven't yet covered what a port actually is. As the name somewhat implies, a port is a way to access a networked service on a computer. Each computer has 65,535 ports that can be either open, or closed at any time. Some services such as HTTP (that serves web pages) or FTP (that allows file transfer) have ports that are associated with them by default. HTTP runs on port 80, FTP runs on port 21, and so on. There are huge lists of commonly used ports that we can reference later — fortunately for us, Nmap has these lists included with its distribution package.

One way to conceptualize a port is to think about an apartment building. In this analogy, one apartment building would be an IP address — each apartment within the building would be a different port. In this case, the building would have to have 65,535 apartments — quite a big property!

When you visit an IP address, it's just like delivering a pizza to the apartment building; you know where it is in the world, but you don't know exactly where you need to be. That's where ports come in! A port is analogous to an apartment number; using a port number, we will know that we're going to 5505 Internet St, Apartment 443, to deliver HTTPS traffic!

Ports are commonly identified by putting a colon after an IP address. If you see an address that looks something like 127.0.0.1:22, then you can safely assume that you are being pointed to the IP address 127.0.0.1 and port 22.

TCP and UDP

One area that is important to understand about networking is the two primary protocols that networked services can use: TCP and UDP. Services can listen on these ports using either of the protocol — and many a times do. TCP (frequently shown as TCP/IP) is used for connections that need things to be ordered specifically — for example, loading a web page. UDP, however, is a connectionless protocol; being connectionless means that UDP connections work like a fire hose of data moving from one IP address (the source address) to another (the destination address). Because of the way the Internet works, though — it is a large packet-switched network — these packets don't always arrive in order. For something like loading a web page, this would be a huge problem. For other uses, however, it makes perfect sense to have data arrive in whatever order it received.

Voice over IP (VoIP) calls, for example, usually use the UDP protocol. It's more important for the data to get to its source, even if a packet is missed or out of order. This way, while there might be a small audible hiccup in the connection, it would not lag while waiting for the data to load. Most of the services that we'll examine in this book are TCP-based, but it's certainly possible to use Nmap to scan UDP services as well (using the -sU flag). UDP does not receive a reply upon successful transmission of a packet, though; so it can be very time-consuming to find out if a service is actually listening on a given UDP port, or simply not replying at all.

Service banners

Now that we understand the very basics of how networks, ports, TCP, and UDP work, we can start to learn the intricacies of Nmap—a powerful tool that leverages various different elements of how computers and networks communicate, to help give us useful information about what services various different computers are running.

The most common use of Nmap—and its original design—was a simple port scanner. A port scanner is simply a piece of software that attempts to connect to each specific target port and see if that port is open—determining whether or not a TCP three-way handshake can be established.

A TCP three-way handshake is a simple way to establish a network-based connection before applications begin to communicate with one another. The structure is very simple—and don't worry if these flags don't mean much to you right now. The three-way handshake, as you might expect, consists of three steps between two speakers (let's call them Alice and Bob). The handshake works as follows:

- Alice is requesting a connection with Bob. Alice sends a **SYN** to Bob at the specified port.
- If Bob wants to establish this connection, Bob sends a response to Alice of **SYN/ACK**.
- Alice receives the **SYN/ACK**, and verifies that the connection is established by sending Bob an **ACK**.

You can visually understand how this works by referring to the following diagram:

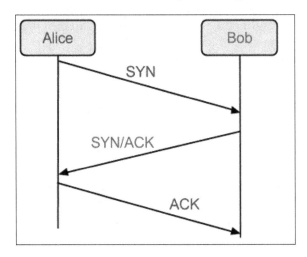

Once you understand how a connection on a certain port is established, it is relatively easy to understand how the most basic Nmap port scan — a SYN scan — works. Nmap sends a **SYN** request to every port in scope (usually either the most common 1,000 ports, or the full 65,535 ports on a host) and waits for a **SYN/ACK** response. If a **SYN/ACK** response is received, then there is a service listening on that open port. Congratulations! We've now covered how basic port scans work. There are many different types of scans — not just SYN scans — but the basic idea of the request/response model should now be fairly clear.

When we're scanning ports, though, we're usually interested in more than just whether or not a port is online. Although most web servers listen on port 80 (which is the HTTP assigned port), someone could just as easily put a web server on port 12345 or 1337. More than just understanding if a port is open, it's important to understand what service is actually listening.

Fortunately for us, Nmap comes with a service version detection module built in. This functionality works by creating a connection to the actual service listening, and looking for a service banner. Nearly every network-based service is identifiable by its initial service banner; even if it's not, though, protocol detection allows Nmap to identify the protocol, if not the exact server version that is running. We will learn how to conduct basic scans — including service version detection — in the next chapter.

Summary

After reading this chapter, you should have a fundamental understanding of how computer networks work. Specifically, it's important to understand how TCP and UDP differ and how port scanning itself functions. Now that you know that the Internet works as a very large computer network—and that you can also scan machines locally on your LAN—you should have a solid foundation to continue learning how Nmap works, and the advanced features that you can use in a plethora of situations.

In the next chapter, we will learn how to conduct a basic Nmap scan in order to get results in the most common situations. This next chapter will get you on your feet and scanning different types of ports and services!

3
Nmap Basics

Now that we understand how networks work, it's time to jump into actually using Nmap to scan computers and networks. This chapter aims to cover several topics that will get you up and running in order to actually scan some of these things.

In this chapter, we will cover:

- How to choose a target
- How to run a default scan
- How to check service versions
- How to log scans (and what the different log types mean)
- How to specify special scan ranges
- How to learn the reasoning for Nmap results

How to choose a target

Although it is generally accepted that scanning computers over the Internet is not a crime, it's also not appreciated by system administrators. There are thousands of scans every second, across all areas of the Internet—but that doesn't mean that you won't get an abuse complaint (or worse) if you scan the wrong machine. Make sure that any target you choose is aware of (and consents to) whatever scan you may decide to conduct. There are a few ways that you can make your own targets—which some readers might find easier than using free ones online.

The most simple target, and easiest to set up, is to just use another computer on your local area network. You can use your router (usually located at 192.168.1.1 for home routers), another machine on your network (which we'll talk about finding), or even buy a cheap laptop to use as a test lab.

If you do not have access to another machine to scan or do not feel comfortable (or authorized) to scan another machine, you can create your own by virtualizing a machine. Although you'll need to be somewhat familiar with installing Linux to make this work, there are free software solutions (such as VirtualBox) and commercial software solutions (such as VMWare or Parallels) to virtualize machines for you. If you decide to take this route to scan targets in this book, I recommend you to install Ubuntu or Debian—you can scan from these machines too! In addition to creating your own virtual server, it's possible to buy a **Virtual Private Server (VPS)** from cloud hosting providers without spending a lot of money. Common providers include Linode, DigitalOcean (which, at the time of writing, has VPSes for only $5 per month), **Amazon Web Services (AWS)**, Rackspace, and so on. The advantage of running one of these cloud-based servers is that you can also get experience in running a fully fledged Linux server. If you are so inclined, you can even host web, email, FTP, or any other service on this server as well!

Lastly, if you do not want to host your own virtual machine, don't have any other machines on your network, and do not want to pay for a virtual private server; you can either scan your own machine (which isn't quite as exciting), or use a free service provided by the Nmap team at `http://scanme.nmap.org/`.

This site gives you full permission to scan, so you do not have to worry about being rude or annoying to any network administrators. On the other hand, it's impossible to actually change any of the services listening on this host, so you can never really change the results you're getting. Using your own computer ("localhost" or 127.0.0.1) can sometimes be a better choice, as you'll be able to run services and see different ports detected.

For the purposes of scanning examples in this book, we will use `http://scanme.nmap.org/` and various additional virtual machines that were set up for the explicit purpose of being scanned. Remember: do not scan without permission!

Running a default scan

Once Nmap is installed and you've chosen a target, it's relatively straightforward to run a scan with the default settings. The command is as straightforward as nmap scanme.nmap.org (assuming http://scanme.nmap.org/ is the target of this particular scan).

```
nmap_book [Running]

dshaw@debian:~$ nmap scanme.nmap.org

Starting Nmap 6.47 ( http://nmap.org ) at 2014-12-11 16:07 PST
Nmap scan report for scanme.nmap.org (74.207.244.221)
Host is up (0.039s latency).
Not shown: 997 filtered ports
PORT      STATE SERVICE
22/tcp    open  ssh
80/tcp    open  http
9929/tcp  open  nping-echo

Nmap done: 1 IP address (1 host up) scanned in 6.83 seconds
dshaw@debian:~$ _
```

As you can see in the preceding screenshot, running a default scan is very easy. Normally, Nmap uses a SYN scan as the default scan type; but because we did not run the scan with root privileges via sudo, Nmap reverts to a "connect" scan instead. We'll get into the differences of specific scan types in *Chapter 4, Advanced Nmap Scans*.

For now, you can see that we've detected three open services. The leftmost column shows the port number and protocol (in this case, 22/tcp, 80/tcp and 9929/tcp) that the port is open and what the service is. When we run Nmap without specifying anything in addition (such as the scan we just ran), the SERVICE column is filled out based on the port specification in /etc/services (on Linux), rather than actually analyzing the protocol. If we want to check the actual service version (by checking banners), we need to specify a different type of scan: the service version scan.

Service version scans

Running a service version scan is very simple; all we need to do is add an additional flag, -sV. This means that we're conducting a service version scan, which can demonstrate which version of each software is running. This is particularly useful if someone is running a service on a non-default port (that does not match up with /etc/services) — in such instances, it's even more important to be able to figure out exactly what's running.

When we run this follow-up scan, you will see that the results are slightly different:

You can see in the preceding screenshot that significantly more information is now being put into the scan results; in this case, we can see the actual patch versions of the OpenSSH, HTTP, and Nping echo services.

In the context of a security assessment, you can see how useful this would be! If you are looking for vulnerabilities in certain versions of software, it's critical to be able to tell exactly what version is running. Vulnerabilities are often only found in specific versions of software (such as between 1.0.1 and 1.0.4), so the granularity of what we see here is very important. It's important to note, however, that if the system administrator restricts the service version, then it is not possible to tell exactly what's running. From a defensive perspective, that is very important!

You might also have noticed that at the top of the scan, before the results, the text Not shown: 997 filtered ports is displayed. Nmap doesn't show all the closed ports in scans, since that would clutter the scan results itself. It's possible to see these (and to see whether they are listed as closed or filtered) by increasing the verbosity of the scan—which we'll get to in *Chapter 4, Advanced Nmap Scans*. However, more importantly, you should remember that there are 65,535 ports that can be opened or closed on every single machine. If we add 997 to the three ports that we already saw were open, we only get 1,000—only a tiny fraction of the total number of ports!

By default, Nmap will only scan the top 1,000 ports that are usually open. This doesn't correspond to the first 1,000 ports, but rather the ones that are most commonly open. You can get the same result by using the --top-ports 1000 flag or specifying a different number (such as --top-ports 200, for example).

Logging scans

Although seeing the results of scans on a case by case basis is very helpful in the short term; for longer assessment times (or for larger scans that would scroll off the screen), it's a good idea to log scans to file.

Nmap supports three different types of logging. Each type has a different flag to log that specific log type, and different purposes. Fortunately for us, the Nmap development team was smart enough to think ahead; using the -oA (output all) flag, it's possible to output all three log files. The second parameter to this flag is simply the base name of the logs. They will automatically have their own unique file extension.

```
dshaw@debian:~$ nmap scanme.nmap.org -oA logbase

Starting Nmap 6.47 ( http://nmap.org ) at 2014-12-11 17:04 PST
Nmap scan report for scanme.nmap.org (74.207.244.221)
Host is up (0.063s latency).
Not shown: 997 filtered ports
PORT      STATE SERVICE
22/tcp    open  ssh
80/tcp    open  http
9929/tcp  open  nping-echo

Nmap done: 1 IP address (1 host up) scanned in 12.58 seconds
dshaw@debian:~$ ls -ltr | grep logbase
-rw-r--r--  1 dshaw dshaw  5451 Dec 11 17:05 logbase.xml
-rw-r--r--  1 dshaw dshaw   384 Dec 11 17:05 logbase.nmap
-rw-r--r--  1 dshaw dshaw   380 Dec 11 17:05 logbase.gnmap
dshaw@debian:~$ _
```

As you can see in the preceding screenshot, Nmap automatically saves all three log file extensions (.xml, .nmap, and .gnmap) with the base file name specified in the -oA flag.

As you can see, after running a scan with the -oA logbase flag, there are now three files in the current directory. We now have a .xml file, which contains the results of the scan (as well as timing details) in XML format, and a .nmap file, which is a human readable output of the scan. In other words, basically the same output that you see on your screen when a scan is run—and also, perhaps most interestingly, a .gnmap file. The .gnmap file stands for **grep-able nmap** output, which is designed to easily be used by the Linux command line tool grep. In other words, it's very easy to search.

```
nmap_book [Running]

dshaw@debian:~$ cat logbase.gnmap | grep open
Host: 74.207.244.221 (scanme.nmap.org)  Ports: 22/open/tcp//ssh///, 80/open/tcp/
/http///, 9929/open/tcp//nping-echo///  Ignored State: filtered (997)
dshaw@debian:~$ cat logbase.gnmap | grep '443/open'
dshaw@debian:~$ _
```

You can easily see in the preceding example that when grepping for "open," we were given the line of the .gnmap file that had open ports. Since we were only scanning one host, the host returned must be the one we scanned—scanme.nmap.org —but in larger scans, it can be extremely useful to figure out which hosts have any open ports (and which we can safely ignore).

Secondly, we did a `grep` for `443/open`. This `grep` didn't return anything (since port 443 was not open in this scan), but you can see how using a greppable output like this can quickly and efficiently determine which hosts had certain ports online. When we talk about active exploitation through Nmap, we'll be able to better understand just how valuable information like this can be.

Specified scan ranges

We learned earlier that by default, Nmap only scans the top 1000 ports. However, services can be put online on any of the 65,535 ports that exist—not just the most common ones. Many system administrators and network engineers run services on very high ports such as 65,001, so that they aren't detected by normal scans. Security through obscurity, though, never really works!

It's possible to specify a specific port range by using the -p flag. So, if you want to only scan port 80 on `scanme.nmap.org`, you can type `nmap -p 80 scanme.nmap.org`. The port specification flag works for ranges too—so, in another example, `nmap -p1-1024 scanme.nmap.org` will scan ports 1 to 1024 (all privileged ports) on the target host.

There's also a useful trick to scan all 65,535 ports on a machine: instead of typing `-p1-65535`, you can simply use the shortcut `-p-`. The Nmap developers were kind and insightful enough to realize that typing the number "65,535" a lot gets quite tiring!

Although we're currently only scanning one host, it's worth noting that there are several ways to specify multiple IP addresses or hostnames as well. CIDR notation (192.168.1.0/24), lists of IP addresses (1.2.3.4,1.2.3.5,1.2.3.6), and targets files (`-iL targets.txt`) are all valid ways to specify hosts to scan. They will all be scanned with the same scan type, and the timing involved is optimized by Nmap itself. We'll talk more about optimizing this process in *Chapter 5, Performance Optimization*.

Understanding the reason flag

Since we've already covered basic networking—including the TCP three-way handshake—in *Chapter 2, Network Fundamentals*, you already know what it means for a port to be `open`, and how that can usually be determined. However, in certain edge cases (and especially for the `filtered` ports), understanding Nmap's logic behind open, closed, and filtered ports can be extremely useful to understand.

You can determine how Nmap reaches its conclusions by using the `--reason` flag.

```
dshaw@debian:~$ nmap --reason -sV scanme.nmap.org

Starting Nmap 6.47 ( http://nmap.org ) at 2014-12-11 17:39 PST
Nmap scan report for scanme.nmap.org (74.207.244.221)
Host is up, received syn-ack (0.064s latency).
Not shown: 997 filtered ports
Reason: 997 no-responses
PORT      STATE SERVICE     REASON  VERSION
22/tcp    open  ssh         syn-ack OpenSSH 5.3p1 Debian 3ubuntu7.1 (Ubuntu Linux;
 protocol 2.0)
80/tcp    open  http        syn-ack Apache httpd 2.2.14 ((Ubuntu))
9929/tcp open   nping-echo syn-ack Nping echo
Service Info: OS: Linux; CPE: cpe:/o:linux:linux_kernel

Service detection performed. Please report any incorrect results at http://nmap.
org/submit/ .
Nmap done: 1 IP address (1 host up) scanned in 15.53 seconds
dshaw@debian:~$ _
```

As demonstrated in the preceding screenshot, a fourth column is now added to the scan after the `--reason` flag is invoked. In this case, we can clearly see that the three services that were identified as online were done so because of syn-ack, indicating a **SYN/ACK** response to a **SYN** request—once we see that a service on a given port is attempting to complete the TCP three-way handshake, we know that there is something listening.

Summary

After reading this chapter, you should be able to conduct many different and interesting types of scans. You should also know how to change the ports you're scanning and how to scan multiple hosts at once. You've learned that grabbing service banners can help you see which versions of software are running, and how to output various different types of log files. Lastly, you should now be able to understand the network-based reasons for why Nmap is flagging results in certain ways. There's a long way to go to become a true Nmap master, but you've conquered the basics of getting a scan under way. In the next chapter, we will learn how to conduct advanced Nmap scans in order to get results in more complex situations. This next chapter will allow you to scan in even strange or hostile environments, which security professionals often encounter during the course of an engagement.

4

Advanced Nmap Scans

You should now be completely able to run Nmap scans against a variety of hosts. That's great! Knowing how to run a basic scan will get you through many situations, but there are a few notable exceptions — and different scan types — that are vital to become a power user.

We will now specifically cover different methods for host detection (so that you know what to scan), how to run scans against devices that are trying to hide themselves, scanning UDP, different verbosity options, and so on.

In this chapter, we will cover:

- Running a ping sweep
- Running a ping agnostic scan
- Scanning UDP services
- Running different TCP flags on scans — such as the Xmas Tree scan
- Operating system detection
- Increasing verbosity in Nmap output
- Showing packet tracing in scans

Host detection methods

In order to scan a host effectively, it's important to first understand how to detect hosts that are "alive" or online. Because many system administrators try to hide their systems from the Internet, certain hosts will appear to be offline until further probed. Fortunately for us, Nmap has several ways to detect which hosts are online.

The most straightforward way to detect hosts is to run a ping sweep. A ping—or an ICMP echo request that machines are designed to respond to—is a simple "are you there?" question and answer conversation.

Pings were named after sonar—the underwater "pings" that submarines send to detect other ships and submersibles in the area—and work in a similar way for computers. While you can test the ping command very easily by simply typing `ping google.com`, using Nmap for ping sweeps can allow significant efficiency gains across larger target network scopes.

It's easy to run a `ping only` sweep with Nmap using the `-sn` flag. This makes sure to run only a ping sweep, rather than a full port scan—which is excellent just to find out which hosts are online.

```
                                                    1. zsh
Nmap scan report for 10.0.0.103
Host is up (0.0027s latency).
Nmap scan report for 10.0.0.106
Host is up (0.0023s latency).
Nmap scan report for 10.0.0.113
Host is up (0.0025s latency).
Nmap scan report for 10.0.0.114
Host is up (0.0037s latency).
Nmap scan report for 10.0.0.118
Host is up (0.0029s latency).
Nmap scan report for 10.0.0.131
Host is up (0.00097s latency).
Nmap scan report for 10.0.0.171
Host is up (0.0031s latency).
Nmap scan report for 10.0.0.177
Host is up (0.0026s latency).
Nmap scan report for 10.0.0.210
Host is up (0.0027s latency).
Nmap scan report for 10.0.0.219
Host is up (0.0018s latency).
Nmap scan report for 10.0.0.220
Host is up (0.0025s latency).
Nmap scan report for 10.0.0.243
Host is up (0.00074s latency).
Nmap scan report for 10.0.0.246
Host is up (0.0032s latency).
Nmap scan report for 10.0.0.249
Host is up (0.0015s latency).
Nmap done: 256 IP addresses (18 hosts up) scanned in 2.67 seconds
dshaw (warpdrive) ~ %
```

In the preceding screenshot, which was run as a `-sn`, (ping sweep) scan, you can clearly see that out of the 256 IP addresses scanned, 18 were "up," or responding to a ping.

Sometimes, however, you need to take this scanning methodology a step further. In order to "hide" from scans, system administrators will often make their systems ignore ping requests. This is often an effective way to hide from network scans!

Running a ping agnostic scan

When a system is hiding from ping sweeps, it can be difficult to know what's online. Fortunately, Nmap provides a ping agnostic method for scanning that can be very beneficial to figure out some of these issues.

When Nmap runs a "normal" scan, it will first run a ping sweep and then follow up with actual port scans (of whatever port ranges specified). If hosts are not responding to a ping, they won't be fully scanned—which means that even if they have services online, those services will not be detected. When running a port scan, missing services or hosts is a very serious problem!

By running a scan with the -Pn flag, Nmap will completely skip running the initial ping sweep, and will scan all hosts in the specified target range. Although this generally takes longer to run—since scanning hosts that are really offline is a big waste of time—it is extremely useful to find hosts that may otherwise have been missed.

```
1. zsh
dshaw (warpdrive) ~ % nmap -Pn -n dshaw.net

Starting Nmap 6.46 ( http://nmap.org ) at 2014-12-22 14:54 PST
Nmap scan report for dshaw.net (173.255.214.88)
Host is up (0.031s latency).
Not shown: 995 closed ports
PORT      STATE SERVICE
22/tcp    open  ssh
25/tcp    open  smtp
80/tcp    open  http
113/tcp   open  ident
9418/tcp  open  git

Nmap done: 1 IP address (1 host up) scanned in 0.51 seconds
dshaw (warpdrive) ~ %
```

You can easily see in the preceding screenshot that dshaw.net—my personal web page, which for the purposes of this scan was configured to not respond to a ping—was still scanned in this ping agnostic scan. When scanning large ranges—such as a Class B network—being able to detect hosts that are trying to appear offline can be invaluable to the security professional.

Although it's not a specific type of scan, it can also be useful to use the Nmap's -sL flag—or the ability to conduct a simple list scan—to either ping or scan the target ranges. This is useful to get reverse DNS lookups, and to understand how many hosts are online in a specified range.

By scanning — or rather by not scanning — this way, excellent results can be achieved.

```
                                              1. zsh
dshaw (warpdrive) ~ % nmap 74.125.224.32-41 -sL

Starting Nmap 6.46 ( http://nmap.org ) at 2014-12-22 14:57 PST
Nmap scan report for lax17s01-in-f0.1e100.net (74.125.224.32)
Nmap scan report for lax17s01-in-f1.1e100.net (74.125.224.33)
Nmap scan report for lax17s01-in-f2.1e100.net (74.125.224.34)
Nmap scan report for lax17s01-in-f3.1e100.net (74.125.224.35)
Nmap scan report for lax17s01-in-f4.1e100.net (74.125.224.36)
Nmap scan report for lax17s01-in-f5.1e100.net (74.125.224.37)
Nmap scan report for lax17s01-in-f6.1e100.net (74.125.224.38)
Nmap scan report for lax17s01-in-f7.1e100.net (74.125.224.39)
Nmap scan report for lax17s01-in-f8.1e100.net (74.125.224.40)
Nmap scan report for lax17s01-in-f9.1e100.net (74.125.224.41)
Nmap done: 10 IP addresses (0 hosts up) scanned in 0.05 seconds
dshaw (warpdrive) ~ %
```

In the preceding screenshot, you can see that the range Nmap "list scanned" points to the 1e100.net domains, which are owned by Google. This is called **zero packet reconnaissance**, since no probes were actually sent to any of the domains in question, but full DNS PTR record lookups were achieved.

The last great Nmap feature that assists in host detection and discovery is the TCP SYN ping scan. Instead of sending an ICMP ping request (which many administrators disable responses to), the TCP SYN scan can treat hosts online if they respond to a SYN request at a given port. For example, if you're scanning a block of IP addresses that usually run SSL web servers, invoking the -PS 443 flag would treat hosts online if there is a response to attempt a connection on port 443. This is extraordinarily useful, and is one of the most valuable features in the Nmap host detection arsenal.

Scanning UDP services

So far we've mentioned UDP services, but haven't talked about how to actually scan them. UDP services are connectionless, which makes scanning them more difficult than traditional port scans — sometimes connections need to be protocol based in order to receive any response, and even when most services receive an actual response, it can take a large amount of time — in other words, scanning UDP services is generally slower and less reliable than their TCP counterparts.

That said, though, it's very important to be able to scan services that only listen on UDP. Many VPNs, for example, have their listening ports as UDP only. NTP and DNS, similarly, often listen exclusively on UDP ports. For this reason, it's important to understand how to scan them.

The caveat here is that it's generally best to do the first "round" of scanning as TCP only and the second sweep as UDP. This is important because having an entire scan forced to wait for UDP responses can make what should have been a five-minute scan, take more than five hours!

The flag to scan UDP services is to simply invoke -sU. Make sure you do so with caution, and when you have plenty of time to spare while waiting for scans!

 As an additional note, UDP scanning does require root privileges in order to run.

```
                                              1. zsh
dshaw (warpdrive) ~ % sudo nmap -sU tick.ucla.edu -p123

Starting Nmap 6.46 ( http://nmap.org ) at 2014-12-22 15:15 PST
Nmap scan report for tick.ucla.edu (164.67.62.194)
Host is up (0.019s latency).
PORT    STATE SERVICE
123/udp open  ntp

Nmap done: 1 IP address (1 host up) scanned in 0.10 seconds
dshaw (warpdrive) ~ %
```

This scan of tick.ucla.edu, a public NTP server, shows that port 123 — **Network Time Protocol (NTP)** — is accepting connections from anywhere on the Internet.

Special TCP scans

We've already covered the two basic scan types that Nmap suggests — TCP connect scans (-sT) and the SYN stealth scan (-sS). These "full" and "half" connection scans will get you through almost any situation, and are absolutely the "go-to" scan types for almost every security professional, system administrator, network engineer, and hobbyist.

However, despite the flexibility that these types of scans can produce, there are occasional reasons to try different flags on packets. For these scans, we will introduce three new scan types: **FIN**, **Xmas Tree**, and **Null** scans.

The driving concept behind running these scans is that a closed port will attempt to reset the connection by issuing a RST (reset) packet, whereas an open port will just drop the connection entirely. This is useful because many **Intrusion Detection Systems (IDS)** are on the lookout for SYN scans — and the stealthy penetration tester never wants to get caught!

```
                                              1. zsh
dshaw (warpdrive) ~ % sudo nmap -sF -n dshaw.net -p80 --reason

Starting Nmap 6.46 ( http://nmap.org ) at 2014-12-22 15:28 PST
Nmap scan report for dshaw.net (173.255.214.88)
Host is up, received echo-reply (0.042s latency).
PORT    STATE           SERVICE REASON
80/tcp open|filtered http      no-response

Nmap done: 1 IP address (1 host up) scanned in 0.52 seconds
dshaw (warpdrive) ~ %
```

The first of these three new options, the FIN scan, starts by sending a FIN packet to each port.

As you can see in the preceding example scan, when running a FIN scan (-sF) against my own web server, there was no response to the FIN request — this makes sense because there is an active service running on port 80 of dshaw.net.

The next scan type is called the Xmas Tree scan — so-called because it is as if a packet is lit up like a Christmas tree! The Xmas Tree scan (-sX) works by flagging FIN, URG, and PUSH flags on a packet header.

The last of these three scan types is the null scan, which sets no flags on the packet header sent to the target port. This scan can be launched by using the -sN option. Make sure that if you're launching a null scan, you capitalize N — otherwise, you'll be accidentally running a ping swing (which we covered in *Host detection methods* section).

Although these scan types can often be very useful, it's worth noting that FIN, Xmas, and NULL scans are known to not work against Microsoft Windows hosts.

Operating system detection

While it's very useful to be able to scan ports—and to use different packet headers in order to produce the best, most accurate results—there are a few things that simple port scanning cannot always achieve reliably. One of the most important of these elements is operating system detection.

When attempting to identify and attack a target, one of the most useful pieces of information is what operating system that machine is running. Because many pieces of software can run on multiple operating systems, this was traditionally a "hard" thing to solve. However, the developers at Nmap—with the help of the information security community at large—have been able to compile a database of the most common (and even some very rare) operating system fingerprints, which can consistently help to identify what operating system a target is running. It's an easy flag to remember—you simply have to invoke a scan with the -o flag.

```
● ● ●                              1. zsh
dshaw (warpdrive) ~ % sudo nmap 10.0.0.10 -O -n

Starting Nmap 6.46 ( http://nmap.org ) at 2014-12-22 15:55 PST
Nmap scan report for 10.0.0.10
Host is up (0.00082s latency).
Not shown: 992 filtered ports
PORT       STATE   SERVICE
22/tcp     closed  ssh
23/tcp     closed  telnet
80/tcp     open    http
443/tcp    open    https
1723/tcp   closed  pptp
8080/tcp   open    http-proxy
49152/tcp  closed  unknown
49153/tcp  closed  unknown
MAC Address: 88:43:E1:AC:5F:C7 (Cisco Systems)
Device type: firewall
Running: Cisco Linux 2.6.X
OS CPE: cpe:/o:cisco:linux_kernel:2.6
OS details: Cisco SA520 firewall (Linux 2.6)
Network Distance: 1 hop

OS detection performed. Please report any incorrect results at http://nmap.org/submit/ .
Nmap done: 1 IP address (1 host up) scanned in 6.62 seconds
dshaw (warpdrive) ~ % █
```

As you can see, this scan of a Cisco security appliance easily identified several parts of the key information. First, we can see the MAC address—and who creates that device. Remember, though, that as we learned in *Chapter 2, Network Fundamentals*, we can only see MAC addresses if we're scanning on a local area network—not over the Internet. Secondly, we can see the OS CPE—and even the OS details: a Cisco SA520 firewall, running the Linux 2.6 kernel. This is absolutely one of the most valuable pieces of information we can pull out of a port scan.

Although it would be wonderful if operating system detection was always as straightforward and concise as it is in this example, which is not the case. The good news, though, is that once you start an operating system scan, Nmap will attempt to gauge how confident it is in the results it gives. In the following example, you can see that although Nmap isn't completely sure what operating system my machine is running (which makes sense when you consider how frequently patches change the way the underlying OS works), it can still give us a pretty good idea!

```
dshaw (warpdrive) ~ % sudo nmap dshaw.net -Pn -O -n

Starting Nmap 6.46 ( http://nmap.org ) at 2014-12-22 16:00 PST
Nmap scan report for dshaw.net (173.255.214.88)
Host is up (0.030s latency).
Not shown: 995 closed ports
PORT     STATE SERVICE
22/tcp   open  ssh
25/tcp   open  smtp
80/tcp   open  http
113/tcp  open  ident
9418/tcp open  git
Aggressive OS guesses: Linux 2.6.39 (95%), Linux 2.6.32 - 2.6.39 (95%), Linux 2.6.32 (93%), Linux 3.4
(93%), Linux 3.1.9 (93%), Linux 2.6.32 - 2.6.35 (91%), Linux 2.6.38 (91%), Fortinet FortiAnalyzer 400B
   firewall (Linux 2.6) (90%), Linux 2.6.32 - 3.0 (90%), Linux 2.6.9 - 2.6.18 (90%)
No exact OS matches for host (test conditions non-ideal).
Network Distance: 10 hops

OS detection performed. Please report any incorrect results at http://nmap.org/submit/ .
Nmap done: 1 IP address (1 host up) scanned in 6.49 seconds
dshaw (warpdrive) ~ %
```

Increasing verbosity in scans

As you have probably noticed throughout the book, more information is almost always better when running scans. Fortunately, Nmap developers allow us to quickly and easily retrieve information about a scan while it's running, by starting the scan with increased verbosity.

Verbosity lets timing, parallelism, and internal debugging information to display straight to the console while scans run. This can be great to figure out when we need to try to optimize scans in one of the several ways (which we'll learn about in the next chapter). When running a scan in increased verbosity, you can also hit *Enter* to see how far the scan has progressed, and how far it has to go before completing its current target file. There are several different levels of verbosity, but I usually use the third-level.

The first level of verbosity gives a very basic information about a scan's progress, and can be invoked by using the -v flag. The second level of verbosity gives more information, including some network and packet information, and can be invoked by using -vv as a flag. Lastly, triple verbosity—which gives out the most information of a scan—can be invoked with the -vvv flag. If you want to make Nmap less verbose than normal, you can also use the --reduce-verbosity flag.

```
1. zsh
dshaw (warpdrive) ~ % sudo nmap dshaw.net -v3 -Pn -p80

Starting Nmap 6.46 ( http://nmap.org ) at 2014-12-22 16:08 PST
Initiating Parallel DNS resolution of 1 host. at 16:08
Completed Parallel DNS resolution of 1 host. at 16:08, 0.01s elapsed
DNS resolution of 1 IPs took 0.01s. Mode: Async [#: 2, OK: 1, NX: 0, DR: 0, SF: 0, TR: 1, CN: 0]
Initiating SYN Stealth Scan at 16:08
Scanning dshaw.net (173.255.214.88) [1 port]
Discovered open port 80/tcp on 173.255.214.88
Completed SYN Stealth Scan at 16:08, 0.03s elapsed (1 total ports)
Nmap scan report for dshaw.net (173.255.214.88)
Host is up (0.025s latency).
rDNS record for 173.255.214.88: code.networkpimps.com
Scanned at 2014-12-22 16:08:57 PST for 0s
PORT    STATE SERVICE
80/tcp open  http

Read data files from: /usr/local/bin/../share/nmap
Nmap done: 1 IP address (1 host up) scanned in 0.09 seconds
        Raw packets sent: 1 (44B) | Rcvd: 1 (44B)
dshaw (warpdrive) ~ % 
```

You can see in the preceding screenshot that on this single-port scan, there is significantly more timing and packet information shown. This can be extremely useful, especially during long scans—such as those that include over 1,000 hosts—to understand better what Nmap is doing at the time. More importantly, this information can be used to determine if timing, parallelism, or other performance adjustments need to be made. For example, if a scan is progressing normally, but only a few hosts are being completed at a time, we know to increase parallelism to make the overall scan go faster. If, however, we're receiving network timeout errors, we know that we're scanning too fast—in that case, we'd want to use a slower timing flag.

Packet tracing

Similar to increasing the verbosity of a scan, it is invaluable to understand the network hops that occur between hosts—and to see the actual network traffic passing through. Although it's possible to use system tools such as **traceroute** and **tcpdump** to find out where on a network target servers land, it can be a painful (and time-consuming) process to do this to many hosts simultaneously.

Instead of using outside tools, Nmap allows packet tracing for each scan—which shows the exact information we need. Instead of looking at this as a security feature (although it certainly does have security-related uses), it's best to think of this as a tool for system administrators and network engineers.

```
                                          1. zsh
dshaw (warpdrive) ~ % sudo nmap dshaw.net --packet-trace -Pn -p80 -n

Starting Nmap 6.46 ( http://nmap.org ) at 2014-12-22 16:23 PST
SENT (0.0411s) TCP 10.0.0.101:40549 > 173.255.214.88:80 S ttl=53 id=57410 iplen=44  seq=1291293169 win
=1024 <mss 1460>
RCVD (0.0680s) TCP 173.255.214.88:80 > 10.0.0.101:40549 SA ttl=56 id=0 iplen=44  seq=1671275609 win=14
600 <mss 1380>
Nmap scan report for dshaw.net (173.255.214.88)
Host is up (0.027s latency).
PORT    STATE SERVICE
80/tcp  open  http

Nmap done: 1 IP address (1 host up) scanned in 0.07 seconds
dshaw (warpdrive) ~ % 
```

This packet tracing example shows tcpdump-style output from Nmap to target machines. Although it doesn't provide excessive value in this simple one-port scan, the information can be great to understand network congestion, packet drop, offline hosts, and so on, on larger scans.

Summary

In this chapter, we covered how to choose a target, run a default scan, check service versions, log scans (and what the different log types mean), specify special scan ranges, and learn the reasoning for Nmap results.

In the next chapter, we will talk about how to ensure your scans are running at peak performance. Nmap has several features that can help scans run quickly, and deliver the results as accurately as possible. Each of these timing, parallelism, and performance improvements will be categorized and explained in the next chapter.

5
Performance Optimization

We are now completely able to scan many different types of hosts, and overcome a plethora of methods that system administrators and network engineers use to defend or mask their machines. Excellent! At this juncture, we will begin to look at some of the broader strokes that Nmap can address: specifically, the difficulty we may encounter if we attempt to scan large swaths of IP addresses that may create performance disruptions.

Unfortunately, using advanced Nmap options, which we learned about in the last chapter, can make scans take significantly longer time than we may have. Performance optimization techniques are some of the least used but most useful Nmap flags, so it's worth it to learn them well — and to employ them when needed.

In this chapter, we will cover:

- Basic Nmap timing optimization
- Customized host group sizes
- How to increase or decrease Nmap's parallelism
- How to deal with stuck hosts
- How to delay (or increase the rate of) individual packets

Nmap timing optimization

The easiest way to make a scan run faster is to use the built-in `timing` flags. These flags are invoked using `-T` and a number from 1 (slowest) to 5 (fastest). The default scanning speed is `-T3`, right in the middle.

There are a few risks to use significantly faster scanning, since it creates certain unreliable aspects in the scan. Particularly, if your network interface is known to be reliable, these options should be used with caution!

The default timing flags change six different elements—many of which we'll go into specific detail, later in this chapter. Specifically, the timing flags change the individual values of `initial_rtt_timeout`, `min_rtt_timeout`, `max_rtt_timeout`, `max_parallelism`, `scan_delay`, and `max_scan_delay`. Don't worry if these flags sound strange to you—we'll cover the different ones you need to know in enough detail that you should be able to debug a large variety of network and performance issues.

Category	Initial_rtt_timeout	min_rtt_timeout	max_rtt_timeout	max_parallelism	scan_delay	max_scan_delay
T0 / Paranoid	5 min	Default (100 ms)	Default (10 sec)	Serial	5 min	Default (1 sec)
T1 / Sneaky	15 sec	Default (100 ms)	Default (10 sec)	Serial	15 sec	Default (1 sec)
T2 / Polite	Default (1 sec)	Default (100 ms)	Default (10 sec)	Serial	400 ms	Default (1 sec)
T3 / Normal	Default (1 sec)	Default (100 ms)	Default (10 sec)	Parallel	Default (0 sec)	Default (1 sec)
T4 / Aggressive	500ms	100ms	1,250ms	Parallel	Default (0 sec)	10ms
T5 / Insane	250ms	50ms	300ms	Parallel	Default (0 sec)	5ms

The preceding screenshot, downloaded from `http://www.professormesser.com/`, shows how the `-T` flags optimize in various different ways. The most important distinctions are the parallel to serial transition between `-T3` and `-T2` (meaning that hosts are no longer scanned at the same time), and the significant time out differences across the board.

System administrators also make the target less vulnerable by increasing the time to respond, as much of the time host information can be read from TTL values, as well.

Running an "insane" scan can clearly make a large network block go faster, but it's interesting to note that on the other end of the spectrum, "sneaky" and "paranoid" scans (`-T1` and `-T0`) can be very effective at "hiding" port scans.

If we are working on a penetration testing engagement with intrusion detection systems and intrusion prevention systems running, it can be very beneficial to run these slow scans.

```
nmap_book [Running]
dshaw@debian:~$ time nmap scanme.nmap.org -p- -T5

Starting Nmap 6.47 ( http://nmap.org ) at 2015-01-06 17:43 PST
Nmap scan report for scanme.nmap.org (74.207.244.221)
Host is up (0.036s latency).
Not shown: 65532 filtered ports
PORT      STATE SERVICE
22/tcp    open  ssh
80/tcp    open  http
9929/tcp  open  nping-echo

Nmap done: 1 IP address (1 host up) scanned in 61.04 seconds

real    1m1.298s
user    0m3.356s
sys     0m19.257s
dshaw@debian:~$ _
```

As you can see in the preceding screenshot, a -T5 scan against scanme.nmap.org (including all ports) took only one minute (and one second), as is visible in the output from the time command and Nmap's own timing calculator. On the other hand, running a -T1 scan—otherwise called "sneaky"—takes significantly longer.

In order to show the true effect of a long-term slow scan, we ran a -T1 scan against the same host—you can see here that after sixteen hours, the scan was still only 2.75% done—that is a very slow scan! It's easy to see how we wouldn't want these scanning options to go through a large block of IP addresses, but that to be extra stealthy on a client engagement (such as one running an IDS or IPS), it could be invaluable.

```
nmap_book [Running]
dshaw@debian:~$ time nmap scanme.nmap.org -p- -T1

Starting Nmap 6.47 ( http://nmap.org ) at 2015-01-06 17:47 PST
Stats: 16:31:32 elapsed; 0 hosts completed (1 up), 1 undergoing Connect Scan
Connect Scan Timing: About 2.75% done; ETC: 18:19 (584:00:14 remaining)
_
```

Customized host group sizes

In order to scan hosts efficiently, Nmap uses groups of hosts that it scans at the same time. Assuming your Internet connection (and computer processing power) is sufficient, it's generally better to increase the host group sizes to finish large scans quickly. For example, if you're scanning 1,000 hosts with a host group size of 250, it will only take four "sweeps" to complete the full scan in parallel.

However, one should carefully weigh what they're looking to achieve by changing the host group sizes. The benefit of scanning many hosts at once is clear, but the downside may not be—if you're scanning a large group, you have to wait for the entire host group to be finished scanning before seeing any results and moving onto another group. If you are trying to see results quickly, a smaller host group would be better for your specific scan.

By default, Nmap tries to take a dynamic middle-ground approach to host group sizes: it dynamically changes the host groups to accommodate a verbose scan (so we can see what's happening) and efficiency (so the full scan finishes quickly). Nmap starts host groups as low as 4 or 5, and increases them to as high as 1024—all automatically.

If you're looking for fine-tuned control, however, there are two host group flags you should keep in mind: `--min-hostgroup` and `--max-hostgroup`. If you're planning to scan a full class C network, for example, specifying a group size of 256 would finish this run-through in one large, parallel pass—greatly increasing the efficiency of the scanning engine.

It's worth noting that host group specification does not work for host discovery scans, including ping sweeps—Nmap will automatically use very large (usually 4096) host groups in order to make these run efficiently.

Increasing and decreasing parallelism

Although the host group size customization we just learned about can help increase or decrease parallelism in full scans, it doesn't deal with the numbers of probes that are being sent out at a time. The actual parallelism flags, however, can help us deal with that!

As with many things, Nmap will attempt to automatically create the most efficient scanning groups, which is great for almost all instances. In my experience, changing the number of simultaneous probes being sent out without having a serious education in networking can result in disaster—but that's not always the case.

By increasing the value of `--min-parallelism`—say up to 10 or 12—you can force Nmap to scan at least that fast. Nmap will still make the scan run faster if it needs to, which reduces some of the risk.

On the other hand, it's possible to set the value of `--max-parallelism` as low as 1. This is very useful; in the sense that you can force Nmap to send out only one probe at a time, but also force the tool to run extremely slowly (as you might imagine). We can use tricks like this to fool security systems, or to ensure that the reliability of our scans are never impacted by network-related issues.

If you see hosts that appear to not be finishing, or you're very concerned with the number of hosts that are scanned in a current group, adjusting parallelism can be very useful.

Dealing with stuck hosts

Unfortunately, when dealing with large blocks of IP addresses—which is a very common occurrence if you're scanning a large enterprise, whether for internal security purposes or as a client engagement—it isn't uncommon to deal with stuck hosts.

When a host gets stuck, it means that something is stopping the scan from completing at a normal rate. This could be caused by something benign such as a network hiccup on either end of the connection, or something more intentional such as a security software that is intentionally making the target host respond very slowly or inconsistently—effectively breaking the scan.

For the purposes of demonstration, I am going to start a ping agnostic (-Pn) scan against a host that doesn't exist on my network. There's no way you can get results from it, but it can still take a very long time to scan.

```
RTTVAR has grown to over 2.3 seconds, decreasing to 2.0
RTTVAR has grown to over 2.3 seconds, decreasing to 2.0
RTTVAR has grown to over 2.3 seconds, decreasing to 2.0
RTTVAR has grown to over 2.3 seconds, decreasing to 2.0
RTTVAR has grown to over 2.3 seconds, decreasing to 2.0
RTTVAR has grown to over 2.3 seconds, decreasing to 2.0
RTTVAR has grown to over 2.3 seconds, decreasing to 2.0
RTTVAR has grown to over 2.3 seconds, decreasing to 2.0
RTTVAR has grown to over 2.3 seconds, decreasing to 2.0
RTTVAR has grown to over 2.3 seconds, decreasing to 2.0
RTTVAR has grown to over 2.3 seconds, decreasing to 2.0
RTTVAR has grown to over 2.3 seconds, decreasing to 2.0
RTTVAR has grown to over 2.3 seconds, decreasing to 2.0
RTTVAR has grown to over 2.3 seconds, decreasing to 2.0
RTTVAR has grown to over 2.3 seconds, decreasing to 2.0
RTTVAR has grown to over 2.3 seconds, decreasing to 2.0
RTTVAR has grown to over 2.3 seconds, decreasing to 2.0
RTTVAR has grown to over 2.3 seconds, decreasing to 2.0
Nmap scan report for 10.0.2.5
Host is up (0.019s latency).
All 65535 scanned ports on 10.0.2.5 are filtered

Nmap done: 1 IP address (1 host up) scanned in 1051.12 seconds
dshaw@debian:~$
```

You can see in the preceding screenshot that it took 1,051 seconds — or seventeen minutes — to scan this non-existent host. Nmap did the best it could to change RTT variables in an attempt to compensate for any network problems, but in the end it took a very long time to realize that nothing was there. Think about what would happen if you were scanning a Class B network! We would be waiting for days, weeks, or years for the scan to complete. No one wants to watch an unresponsive Nmap screen!

```
dshaw@debian:~$ nmap -Pn -p- 10.0.2.5 --host-timeout 1m

Starting Nmap 6.47 ( http://nmap.org ) at 2015-01-07 15:43 PST
RTTVAR has grown to over 2.3 seconds, decreasing to 2.0
RTTVAR has grown to over 2.3 seconds, decreasing to 2.0
RTTVAR has grown to over 2.3 seconds, decreasing to 2.0
RTTVAR has grown to over 2.3 seconds, decreasing to 2.0
RTTVAR has grown to over 2.3 seconds, decreasing to 2.0
RTTVAR has grown to over 2.3 seconds, decreasing to 2.0
RTTVAR has grown to over 2.3 seconds, decreasing to 2.0
RTTVAR has grown to over 2.3 seconds, decreasing to 2.0
RTTVAR has grown to over 2.3 seconds, decreasing to 2.0
RTTVAR has grown to over 2.3 seconds, decreasing to 2.0
RTTVAR has grown to over 2.3 seconds, decreasing to 2.0
RTTVAR has grown to over 2.3 seconds, decreasing to 2.0
RTTVAR has grown to over 2.3 seconds, decreasing to 2.0
RTTVAR has grown to over 2.3 seconds, decreasing to 2.0
Nmap scan report for 10.0.2.5
Host is up (3.0s latency).
Skipping host 10.0.2.5 due to host timeout
Nmap done: 1 IP address (1 host up) scanned in 60.12 seconds
dshaw@debian:~$
```

In this second scan against a host that doesn't exist, we kept the same flags, but changed `--host-timeout` to 1 minute. As you can see, after 60 seconds, Nmap gave up on the host and finished the scan—one seventeenth of the time it would have taken to complete!

The `--host-timeout` flag is very useful, especially in large scans, but make sure that you don't set the time too low—or Nmap will give up on hosts that it was still actively scanning! In many assessments, my team will set `--host-timeout` to 10 minutes, which generally is enough time for many port scans to complete without any error per host. Combined with parallelism and host group customization, setting a host time out flag can save significant amounts of time on larger target hosts.

Delaying and increasing probe rates

The last important timing improvement flag to understand is delaying and increasing rates directly. This is probably the most fine-tuned of the performance optimization, and should generally only be used if there is a specific problem you are trying to solve, or a situation you are trying to create.

The first of these flags, `--scan-delay`, specifies the amount of time that Nmap should wait, not doing anything, between probes. This can be extremely useful in slowing scans down (and sometimes speeding them up, with a low scan-delay). Again, the most common usage of slowing down scans is to avoid detection of a target administrator or security system, or to try to avoid network throttling issues. Since many systems use the rate at which requests are being made to determine whether or not the machine is under attack, this can be a very stealthy technique without very much effort on the part of the tester. It's also useful to note that `--max-scan-delay` can be used in conjunction with other timing flags to supersede them, and ensure that scan delays are never slower than a certain amount of time.

```
nmap_book (Running)
dshaw@debian:~$ nmap scanme.nmap.org --scan-delay 5s -p22,80,3389,8080

Starting Nmap 6.47 ( http://nmap.org ) at 2015-01-07 16:13 PST
Nmap scan report for scanme.nmap.org (74.207.244.221)
Host is up (0.030s latency).
PORT     STATE    SERVICE
22/tcp   open     ssh
80/tcp   open     http
3389/tcp filtered ms-wbt-server
8080/tcp filtered http-proxy

Nmap done: 1 IP address (1 host up) scanned in 41.29 seconds
dshaw@debian:~$ _
```

You can see in the preceding screenshot that increasing `--scan-delay` to 5 seconds made a four-port scan (plus ping sweep) take 41 seconds. Not great for efficiency, but perfect to conceal what's happening!

Lastly, direct control of Nmap's rates can also be set using a combination of `--min-rate` and `--max-rate`, which controls the packets per second sent over the network. It's worth noting that Nmap's internal controls for these settings are very good, but on occasion, more fine-tuned control is necessary. By setting flags such as `--min-rate 1` and `--max-rate 100`", we can allow Nmap's built-in timing engine to control efficiency — but never send more than 100 packets per second or less than 1 per second. As with many of these flags, it's important to never set the minimum value too high or the maximum value too low!

Summary

This chapter taught us some very valuable timing flags — Nmap is versatile enough to include many options that can help us make sure we have complete control over timing, in order to maximize efficiency and overcome potential pitfalls.

In this chapter, we covered basic Nmap timing optimization, customized host group sizes, how to increase or decrease Nmap's parallelism, how to deal with stuck hosts, and how to delay (or increase the rate of) individual packets.

In the next chapter, we will talk about one of the most interesting and powerful features of Nmap: the **Nmap Scripting Engine** (**NSE**). We'll talk about what the NSE is, what it can do, and how to invoke interesting scripts using it.

6

Introduction to the Nmap Scripting Engine

Although being able to conduct port scans is an integral part of using the Nmap suite of tools, the developers of Nmap created a very powerful engine that's built into the tool: the **Nmap Scripting Engine** (**NSE**). This chapter introduces the NSE, and covers all the topics needed to use reliably-written scripts in the Nmap script repository, in order to conduct reconnaissance scans that include much more than just what ports are open and which services are listening.

In this chapter, we will cover:

- The history of the NSE
- How the NSE works
- How to find existing scripts to use
- How to run scripts using the NSE

The history of the NSE

By the mid-2000s, Nmap had established itself as the clear leader in port scanning tools — and security tools in general — whether open source or not. Although it's a constant battle to continually innovate and optimize, Nmap can only be considered as an extremely successful project.

Due to its popularity, and the fact that it's an open source project with a relatively high profile, Nmap was selected to participate in Google Summer of Code several times. Google Summer of Code is a software development internship/association project, during which students are selected and put on open source software teams to build new features into existing projects.

In May 2006—when the currently released version of Nmap was only 4.0—Nmap was selected for its second Summer of Code season. The previous year, in 2005, several improvements had been made through the students' coding for the Nmap project: the students had written a contemporary implementation of Netcat (called Ncat), upgraded the OS detection for Nmap to its second (and much better) generation, and created a small, simplified GUI that would later become Zenmap.

For this second run through, after an extremely successful first summer, the participant developers were even more ambitious. Since Nmap clearly had an excellent set of features, why not make those features extendable by the greater community? New vulnerabilities and scanning techniques were being pioneered on a very frequent basis, and full Nmap releases couldn't keep up with the things that security professionals needed to assess. Every time a new vulnerability came out, security professionals (and malicious hackers!) would scan for vulnerable services with Nmap, but could only test whether software versions were vulnerable by using manual analysis: clearly, not a very efficient use of time.

Because of the new resources granted by Google Summer of Code developers, an arbitrary scripting framework was created that allows users to trigger additional checks based on certain open ports or services. This means, for example, that if you're looking for a specific file on all web servers—`robots.txt`, for example— you can easily create a script that can check for it on all HTTP and HTTPS services. The NSE (and the inclusion of Nmap scripts in default installations of Nmap) truly revolutionized the versatility of the tool suite.

After months of hard work, the NSE was released in December 2006, packaged with Nmap release 4.21ALPHA1. The scripts that come packaged with the NSE have continued to grow in complexity and usability, and are excellent resources to turn Nmap into a fully-featured security tool suite.

The inner working of the NSE

The NSE is a framework that runs code written in the programming language Lua with specific flags that the engine can parse. Lua is a lightweight, fast, and interpreted programming language—one that has the most fame for scripting user interfaces for computer games such as *World of Warcraft*—that has a similar syntax to other contemporary interpreted languages.

If you've ever seen code written in Python or Ruby, Lua won't seem too alien to you.

```
portrule = shortport.port_or_service(8333, "bitcoin", "tcp" )

action = function(host, port)

  local NETWORK = {
    [3652501241] = "main",
    [3669344250] = "testnet"
  }

  local bcoin = bitcoin.Helper:new(host, port, { timeout = 10000 })
  local status = bcoin:connect()

  if ( not(status) ) then
    return "\n  ERROR: Failed to connect to server"
  end

  local status, ver = bcoin:exchVersion()
  if ( not(status) ) then
    return "\n  ERROR: Failed to extract version information"
  end
  bcoin:close()

  local result = {}
  table.insert(result, ("Timestamp: %s"):format(stdnse.format_timestamp(ver.timestamp)))
  table.insert(result, ("Network: %s"):format(NETWORK[ver.magic]))
  table.insert(result, ("Version: %s"):format(ver.ver))
  table.insert(result, ("Node Id: %s"):format(ver.nodeid))
  table.insert(result, ("Lastblock: %s"):format(ver.lastblock))

  return stdnse.format_output(true, result)
end
```

The preceding screenshot shows an Nmap script that identifies information about Bitcoins (written by Patrik Karlsson). Don't worry if you don't understand it yet—that's something we will cover in *Chapter 7, Writing Nmap Scripts*—but you can see that the code used to generate a relatively complex Nmap script looks very simple. This is the whole point of the NSE! Where security engineers and system administrators used to have to export Nmap results, find the information they are looking for and then use third-party tools to assist them; they are now able to either find a script that serves their purposes, or write a simple one themselves. Many penetration testers can leverage the Nmap scripting language to even weaponize the tool for security exploits—which we will cover in more detail in *Chapter 10, Penetration Testing with Metasploit*.

Finding Nmap scripts

Many Nmap scripts come with Nmap, and are already prepackaged on your system. Still, though, it can be difficult to determine which scripts you'd like to run for each particular scan—or assessment—that you may be on. Fortunately, the NSE documentation portal is one of the most in-depth and well-documented aspects of the entire Nmap project.

 By going to http://nmap.org/nsedoc/, you can see all of the scripts that are part of the official Nmap script repository.

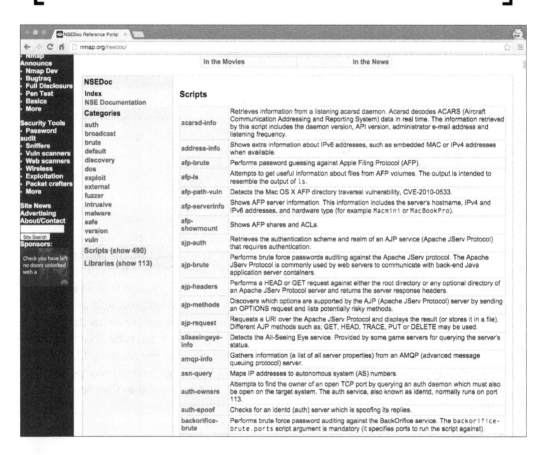

The preceding screenshot shows the **Nmap Scripting Engine Documentation** (**NSEDoc**) reference portal web page, as well as all the official Nmap scripts at the time of writing this book. Each script has a small paragraph next to its name, which gives a brief description of what it is designed to do. At the time of writing, there are 490 and 113 Nmap scripts that are part of the official documentation — that's quite a lot you can do with the NSE!

These scripts are broken down into several categories, each with their own specific use case. It's worth noting that sometimes these scripts can be in several categories, depending on the full functionality of the script. The categories and their definitions are as follows:

- **Auth**: These scripts attempt to authenticate to services, and can verify found credentials

- **Broadcast**: These scripts broadcast certain protocols in order to find out whether or not they are listening

- **Brute**: These scripts attempt brute force or dictionary-based attacks against network services

- **Default**: This is the default category of scripts that may run when a scan is initiated

- **Discovery**: These scripts attempt to enumerate sensitive information from hosts and network services

- **Denial of Service (DoS)**: These scripts may cause disruption to the service that is being scanned

- **Exploit**: These scripts attempt to execute an exploit that exploits a given vulnerability

- **External**: These scripts query third-party databases, such as DNS blacklists, to gather additional information about targets

- **Fuzzer**: These scripts send random "garbage" information to services in order to attempt to find flaws in the software

- **Intrusive**: These scripts are an umbrella category for any script that may cause damage or be intrusive to the service itself

- **Malware**: These scripts attempt to find instances of the known malware.

- **Safe**: These scripts are verified to not cause harm to servers

- **Version**: These scripts attempt to identify specific versions — as well as information disclosures — from specific services in a more in-depth way than normal service version detection

- **Vuln**: These scripts identify the known vulnerabilities in services

It's important to know which categories you want to run, since several of these categories — specifically DoS, exploit, and intrusive — can be dangerous to run against weak or production systems. The inclusion of these Nmap scripts in security assessments can easily increase the utility of Nmap in a very significant way.

Running Nmap scripts

Running Nmap scripts is easy — and some, the "default" category, will even run on their own as a part of a normal scan. Some scripts are designed to simply give additional information about a target, while others will go so far as to actively exploit it (the "exploit" category) or even take it offline (the "DoS" category).

The first step to run an Nmap script that's part of the actually NSEDoc repository is to verify that the script is stored locally. Unlike the Nmap tool itself, the Nmap script repository is frequently updated — so it's in your best interest to always verify that you have the most updated version. You can update the NSE scripts by running Nmap with the flag `--script-updatedb`, which updates the script database.

```
dshaw@debian:~$ sudo nmap --script-updatedb

Starting Nmap 6.47 ( http://nmap.org ) at 2015-01-19 16:36 PST
NSE: Updating rule database.
NSE: Script Database updated successfully.
Nmap done: 0 IP addresses (0 hosts up) scanned in 2.18 seconds
dshaw@debian:~$ _
```

Once the script database is updated, you can select scripts by using the --script tag. You can either select specific scripts for a given purpose, or you can select broad categories of scripts. Fortunately, the Nmap developers allow categories of scripts to be selected at once. For example, let's say that we wanted to run all scripts that are default, but also all scripts that are intrusive; we can run a scan using the --script default or intrusive flag:

```
nmap_book [Running]
dshaw@debian:~$ sudo nmap scanme.nmap.org --script default

Starting Nmap 6.47 ( http://nmap.org ) at 2015-01-19 17:29 PST
Nmap scan report for scanme.nmap.org (74.207.244.221)
Host is up (0.0087s latency).
Not shown: 997 filtered ports
PORT     STATE SERVICE
22/tcp   open  ssh
80/tcp   open  http
|_http-title: Go ahead and ScanMe!
9929/tcp open  nping-echo

Nmap done: 1 IP address (1 host up) scanned in 8.05 seconds
dshaw@debian:~$ _
```

You can see in the preceding screenshot that running default scripts here clearly flagged several findings immediately. If you were to run the same scan with -vv to have double-verbose mode enabled on the scan, you would also be able to see the number of scripts loaded against the given target (in this case, 93). In this particular instance, the http-title script showed the HTML title (Go ahead and ScanMe!) in the scan results itself.

If selecting scans by category or categories is too much, you can also select scans by their specific name, or use wildcards. For example, if I wanted to scan a web server and load all the HTTP modules in the default scan repository, I would scan with the `--script "http-*"` flag:

```
dshaw@debian:~$ sudo nmap scanme.nmap.org --script "http-*"

Starting Nmap 6.47 ( http://nmap.org ) at 2015-01-19 17:32 PST
Pre-scan script results:
| http-icloud-findmyiphone:
|_   ERROR: No username or password was supplied
| http-icloud-sendmsg:
|_   ERROR: No username or password was supplied
_
```

You can see that launching a scan with the `"http-*"` wildcard script name works in loading every script, but there are a few errors coming up. Certain scripts take parameters, so if loading many scripts, it's important to understand which ones are being loaded. The scripts that could accurately fire at HTTP ports will still launch, but those that require additional information would fail (and not return any useful information). To provide additional information to Nmap scripts, you can provide arguments with the `--script-args` flag.

Lastly, it's possible to combine different options to launch scripts by including different tags in parenthetical. For example, if you wanted to launch scripts that fit into the categories of default, safe, or intrusive — but specifically did not want to launch any scripts that launch against web servers — you could start a scan with the `--script` (default, safe, or intrusive) flag and not `"http-*"`. Always remember to keep in mind that the `or` flag is not an exclusive or — meaning that scripts in both categories will still run — but `and` must be in both sections.

Although the Nmap script repository is very thorough, it's always worth looking elsewhere on the Internet if a specific script that you think would be useful is not published. Many blogs from security researchers will have NSE scripts for a specific purpose, and before trying to write your own, it's absolutely worth it to check a search engine first!

Summary

This chapter introduced the NSE, which can be one of the most useful, versatile, and engaging features of the Nmap tool suite. We should now be able to launch scans that do more than just port and service versions—Nmap scripts can actually interact with the services listening, and in some cases can even exploit vulnerabilities!

In this chapter ,we covered the history of the NSE, how NSE works, how to find existing scripts to use, and how to run scripts using the NSE.

In the next chapter, we will learn how to write a basic Nmap script using Lua. Although many, many scripts already exist for a huge variety of tasks, custom in-house uses may require writing one of our own.

7
Writing Nmap Scripts

Now that we have covered how the NSE works, it's time to learn how to write our first Nmap script. Because of the versatile and extremely customized nature of writing Nmap scripts, there are several different ways to produce a script that performs various functions—and also many pros and cons to write your own script.

While creating an Nmap script from scratch may not always be the fastest way to get things done (as there is almost always a script that already exists for whatever purpose you may need), there are certain situations during which leveraging the powerful built-in functions of the Nmap scripting engine leads to exactly the right circumstances to write your own script.

In this chapter, we will cover the following topics:

- The anatomy of an Nmap script
- Writing the Nmap script's head
- Creating a rule
- Defining a script's action
- Debugging Nmap scripts

Anatomy of an Nmap script

An Nmap script is comprised of several unique sections, each of which define different areas for the script to execute, or for Nmap to interpret expected output. There are several primary areas that we must always include in any script we create, in order to ensure that the script will run effectively (and that Nmap will be able to understand how to interpret the data).

Although Nmap scripts are written in Lua, an interpreted programming language, it's important to remember that these scripts are not stand-alone executables that can be run on their own. Rather than running a script with Nmap as a requirement, it's better to think of Nmap scripts as simply sets of instructions for a unique Nmap programming language.

An Nmap script is comprised of three unique sections:

- **The head**: This section of an Nmap script includes documentation and categorization for the script so that Nmap and the NSE database can successfully categorize the script into the appropriate areas.

- **The rule**: This section of the script defines exactly where and how an Nmap script is executed. Because the script is leveraging the data of the Nmap scan as it runs, certain elements can trigger the script to run. This is effectively a trigger that evaluates whether or not the script should execute.

- **The action**: Lastly, this section of an Nmap script is where (you guessed it!) the action takes place. This is the part of the script that is doing a lot of the processing, after the head has defined the script and the rule has triggered the action.

Now that we've learned how an Nmap script is composed, it's time that we got to work and started writing one. Because each and every Nmap script is so unique, we are going to recreate a script that already works—but the one that shows how powerful the NSE can be.

Our case study for this script will be to write a simple, easy-to-follow Nmap script that uses Nmap's built-in functionality (combined with the power of the NSE) to determine whether a web server has a `robots.txt` file. The `robots.txt` files indicate which areas of a website should (and should not) be indexed by web crawlers and search engines, and often have sensitive directories listed with an instruction to not index them. For this reason, they're very interesting for security professionals and penetration testers—since it's exactly those sensitive files and directories that we're looking for!

Defining an Nmap script – script headers

Each Nmap script must be created with certain required variables defined at the beginning of the script. Any Nmap prerequisites that are needed for successful execution, definitions of how the script is categorized (for example, whether or not it is intrusive, safe, contains an exploit, and so on), and the license are also among the things necessary in the header.

```
local brute = require "brute"
local creds = require "creds"
local http = require "http"
local nmap = require "nmap"
local shortport = require "shortport"
local string = require "string"
local table = require "table"
local stdnse = require "stdnse"

description = [[
Performs brute force password auditing against http basic authentication.
]]


---
-- @usage
-- nmap --script http-brute -p 80 <host>
--
-- This script uses the unpwdb and brute libraries to perform password
-- guessing. Any successful guesses are stored in the nmap registry, under
-- the nmap.registry.credentials.http key for other scripts to use.
--
-- @output
-- PORT     STATE SERVICE REASON
-- 80/tcp   open  http    syn-ack
-- | http-brute:
-- |   Accounts
-- |     Patrik Karlsson:secret => Valid credentials
-- |   Statistics
-- |_    Perfomed 60023 guesses in 467 seconds, average tps: 138
--
-- Summary
-- -------
--   x The Driver class contains the driver implementation used by the brute
--     library
--
-- @args http-brute.path points to the path protected by authentication (default: <code>/</code>)
-- @args http-brute.hostname sets the host header in case of virtual hosting
-- @args http-brute.method sets the HTTP method to use (default: <code>GET</code>)
--
--
-- Version 0.1
-- Created 07/30/2010 - v0.1 - created by Patrik Karlsson <patrik@cqure.net>
-- Version 0.2
-- 07/26/2012 - v0.2 - added digest auth support (Piotr Olma)
--

author = "Patrik Karlsson, Piotr Olma"
license = "Same as Nmap--See http://nmap.org/book/man-legal.html"
categories = {"intrusive", "brute"}
```

The preceding screenshot illustrates the various sections necessary for an Nmap script, each of which are critical to the successful execution of the program. Let's walk through these elements in order to determine what the author of the script is doing.

First, several variables (defined by the local prefix) are defined. Several requirements are made in order to ensure that each of the Nmap elements are included appropriately.

Next, a longer variable — the description — is created. This is a multiline Lua variable, which is encapsulated in [[and]] brackets. This area is supposed to include a basic description of the Nmap script so that when run programmatically, it is possible to choose the correct script.

Below the description variable is a fully commented text block that defines the usage of the script. In Lua, the -- preamble comments out that line of code, making it not run when the script is executed. You can easily see how the @usage block is formatted— simply showing how the script should be run, and any arguments it may accept—and how the @output block is formatted below. These blocks show how to run the script correctly, how to pass arguments on the command line (if any are required), and what output you should expect from the script in question.

Below the commented out block are several other variable definitions that Nmap parses. Specifically, the author block (which is how you would like to be credited for the script), the license block (which is generally listed as the same as Nmap for distribution purposes, but can be specified in certain ways if you want to protect certain elements of your script), and the categories array (which lists the categories that the script should fall into). You want to make sure that, for example, if your script is intrusive, you label it as such.

For our script, we only need a few required includes, which make our header relatively short. Let's create our head section, looking something like the following (of course, feel free to modify your script however you like!):

```
local http = require "http"
local nmap = require "nmap"

description = [[
Checks to see if robots.txt exists on a web server.
]]

author = "Nmap Essentials readers"
license = "Same as Nmap--See http://nmap.org/book/man-
    legal.html"
categories = {"default", "discovery", "safe"}
```

Very simple! We need the HTTP module in order to perform an HTTP GET request to robots.txt in question (on an open port 80), and of course we need the Nmap include in order to leverage the Nmap scripting engine. You can see that our description is very straightforward, and we defined the author, license, and categories in order to help our users determine when the script is safe and effective to run.

Now that the head of our script is complete, let's turn to the rule.

Triggering functions – the rule

The rule or portrule section of an Nmap script determines when the action should take place (which we'll cover in the next section). It's important to define this clearly so that we are confident that our script will run every time we need it to (based on port number and version). There are two ways to accomplish this type of rule: standard portrule documentation, and a helper library built in the NSE called **shortport**.

Defining a rule is actually very simple, depending on what we're looking for. In the case of our `robots.txt` detection script (aptly named `robots.nse`), we just want to trigger on port 80 to see if `robots.txt` exists.

If we were writing a production script, rather than a proof of concept, it would probably be a good idea to use shortport's port or service functionality to trigger on port 80, or any web server that Nmap detects through its underlying functionality. However, in our case, we can simply define something much easier to digest:

```
portrule = function(host, port)
   return port.state == "open"
end
```

As you can see, this is a very minimal portrule that will return `true` when `port.state` is `open`. These are built-in Nmap functionalities, and when the script is running, each port is checked against the portrule.

While our portrule is intentionally very easy to understand, many production scripts have very complicated portrules that are designed to trigger different elements of analysis, based on specific version and configuration settings. To learn more about advanced portrule and the shortport library, you can read the full overviews at the **Nmap Scripting Engine Documentation** (**NSEDoc**) portal.

Defining a script's action

After we define the portrule, the only step left is to define the action that executes when the portrule returns `true`. In our case, we want to check whether `robots.txt` exists on the web server we're scanning.

In order to determine whether the server exists, there's a little bit about the **Hypertext Transfer Protocol (HTTP)** that we need to learn. First of all, the way to request a page is through an HTTP GET request. For example, if we wanted to go to `http://google.com/images`, our browser would send a request containing `GET /images` to the server at `Google.com`.

If the status of the GET request is OK, the web server returns the status code 200. If there is a server-side error, a 500 error will return. If the page is moved, an error in the range of 300 will return. Lastly (for our purposes), if there is an authorization error or file-not-found error, the server will return 403 or 404 respectively.

In order to define our action function, we need to perform the following steps:

1. Request the robots.txt page.
2. Find out whether it's there or not.

The following action segments define this request:

```
action = function(host, port)
local robots = http.get(host, port, "/robots.txt")

if robots.status == 200 then
  return "robots.txt status 200"
else
  return "robots.txt status: " .. robots.status
end
end
```

As you can see in the preceding code snippet, this is a very simple action section. Let's walk through the process step by step:

1. First, we define the action function that takes the parameter's host and port. These are automatically passed to the action block once the portrule triggers.
2. Next, we define a local variable (called robots), which is the HTTP result of the NSE's http.get request. In this instance, we're performing a GET to the host and port that we're currently scanning and making a request to /robots.txt.
3. Once we receive the HTTP data, we can easily make an if statement to determine whether the status is a 200 OK response or something else. We could have combined this with a shorter if statement (rather than an if/else), but it's useful to see how to have multiple possibilities for output.
4. If the output is not 200, we go to the else statement and see what the status is. For example, if the status is 404, we know that it simply doesn't exist; if we get a 500 server error or a 403 not authorized, however, it might be worth looking into a greater depth:

```
dshaw (warpdrive) ~ % nmap scanme.nmap.org -p80 --script robots.nse

Starting Nmap 6.46 ( http://nmap.org ) at 2015-02-02 17:59 PST
Nmap scan report for scanme.nmap.org (74.207.244.221)
Host is up (0.026s latency).
PORT    STATE SERVICE
80/tcp open  http
|_robots: robots.txt status: 404

Nmap done: 1 IP address (1 host up) scanned in 0.93 seconds
dshaw (warpdrive) ~ % ▮
```

As you can see, running this script (and any custom Nmap script) is very
straightforward. When scanning scanme.nmap.org, you can clearly see that there
is no robots.txt — we're just receiving a 404 error. If we scan a service that does
have a robots.txt page — I created a test case on http://dshaw.net/ for this
purpose — we see a different result.

In this instance, we can clearly see that the 200 status — HTTP OK — means that
robots.txt does exist:

```
dshaw (warpdrive) ~ % nmap dshaw.net -p80 --script robots.nse -n

Starting Nmap 6.46 ( http://nmap.org ) at 2015-02-02 18:10 PST
Nmap scan report for dshaw.net (173.255.214.88)
Host is up (0.039s latency).
PORT    STATE SERVICE
80/tcp open  http
|_robots: robots.txt status 200

Nmap done: 1 IP address (1 host up) scanned in 0.20 seconds
dshaw (warpdrive) ~ % ▮
```

If this were a production Nmap script, it would probably be worth it to change the return associated with a `200 OK` response to show more information such as disallowed files and directories. However, don't spend time on this particular script! There is already a great HTTP `robots.txt` script (and many more) in the official Nmap repository.

One last set of flags that can be very useful to write, understand, and debug Nmap scripts are the `--script-trace` and `-d` (debug) flags. The `--script-trace` flag shows the information on the wire about all the different requests that the script is making on its own, which is very useful to determine what exactly is happening:

```
[173.255.214.88:80] (203 bytes)
NSE: TCP 10.0.0.101:55514 < 173.255.214.88:80 | 00000000: 48 54 54 50 2f 31 2e 31 20 3
2 30 30 20 4f 4b 0d HTTP/1.1 200 OK
00000010: 0a 53 65 72 76 65 72 3a 20 6e 67 69 6e 78 0d 0a   Server: nginx
00000020: 44 61 74 65 3a 20 54 75 65 2c 20 30 33 20 46 65   Date: Tue, 03 Fe
00000030: 62 20 32 30 31 35 20 30 32 3a 32 32 3a 33 37 20 b 2015 02:22:37
00000040: 47 4d 54 0d 0a 43 6f 6e 74 65 6e 74 2d 54 79 70   GMT   Content-Typ
00000050: 65 3a 20 74 65 78 74 2f 70 6c 61 69 6e 0d 0a 43 e: text/plain  C
00000060: 6f 6e 74 65 6e 74 2d 4c 65 6e 67 74 68 3a 20 34 ontent-Length: 4
00000070: 0d 0a 4c 61 73 74 2d 4d 6f 64 69 66 69 65 64 3a   Last-Modified:
00000080: 20 54 75 65 2c 20 30 33 20 46 65 62 20 32 30 31   Tue, 03 Feb 201
00000090: 35 20 30 32 3a 30 35 3a 34 30 20 47 4d 54 0d 0a 5 02:05:40 GMT
000000a0: 43 6f 6e 6e 65 63 74 69 6f 6e 3a 20 63 6c 6f 73 Connection: clos
000000b0: 65 0d 0a 41 63 63 65 70 74 2d 52 61 6e 67 65 73 e  Accept-Ranges
000000c0: 3a 20 62 79 74 65 73 0d 0a 0d 0a               : bytes

NSOCK INFO [0.2760s] nsock_read(): Read request from IOD #1 [173.255.214.88:80] (timeo
ut: 8000ms) EID 34
NSOCK INFO [0.2760s] nsock_trace_handler_callback(): Callback: READ SUCCESS for EID 34
 [173.255.214.88:80] (4 bytes): lol.
NSE: TCP 10.0.0.101:55514 < 173.255.214.88:80 | 00000000: 6c 6f 6c 0a
                   lol

NSE: TCP 10.0.0.101:55514 > 173.255.214.88:80 | CLOSE
NSOCK INFO [0.2760s] nsi_delete(): nsi_delete (IOD #1)
Nmap scan report for dshaw.net (173.255.214.88)
Host is up (0.028s latency).
PORT   STATE SERVICE
80/tcp open  http
|_robots: robots.txt status 200

Nmap done: 1 IP address (1 host up) scanned in 0.28 seconds
dshaw (warpdrive) ~ %
```

You can see in the preceding screenshot that while there may be a little bit of information overload, you can see exactly what the Nmap script is doing by using the `--script-trace` flag. The `-d` flag, to debug, works similarly: if you're writing a script and you encounter errors, try debugging it with the `-d` flag. You'd be surprised at the great things you can learn!

Summary

This chapter showed us how to write our very own Nmap scripts! The NSE is a powerful (and sometimes complicated) tool, which can aid Nmap users in a variety of interesting and automated tasks. The script we wrote as a proof of concept can easily detect whether a `robots.txt` file exists on a server, but the possibilities to write Nmap scripts—either for internal use, or to detect specific vulnerabilities—are nearly endless!

In the next chapter, we will learn how to use tools that come in packages with the Nmap tool suite, as well as some useful tips and tricks to get the most out of them.

8
Additional Nmap Tools

We have now successfully written our first Nmap script, and launched a variety of scans against a plethora of different target types (and defenses). However, scanning a host is only a small part of the full power of the Nmap suite.

In addition to creating a powerful scanning tool and the NSE, Nmap developers have included several additional tools—including Ncrack, Nping, Ncat, and Ndiff—into default install bundles of Nmap. These tools can help analyze existing scans, pivot to other hosts, transfer files, or compare scan results over time.

In this chapter, we will cover the following topics:

- Attacking services with Ncrack
- Host detection with Nping
- File transfers and backdoors with Ncat
- Comparing Nmap results with Ndiff

Attacking services with Ncrack

One of the most aggressive tools included in the Nmap suite is Ncrack—a tool for aggressively brute-forcing (or "cracking") network services. While it's not unique in its functionality (as there are many software tools that can brute force network accounts), the ability to easily (and natively) integrate with Nmap (and Nmap results) makes it ideal for use after scans.

Before using Ncrack, we need to ensure that it's installed. Although most Nmap tools come installed with Nmap suite packages, since Ncrack is technically (at the time of writing) an alpha build, it is not included in many installations.

[Documentation and the most recent download link is available at
`http://nmap.org/ncrack/`.]

Installation, like many Nmap tools, is extraordinarily simple; perform the
following steps:

1. `wget http://nmap.org/ncrack/dist/ncrack-0.4ALPHA.tar.gz`

2. `tar -xzf ncrack-0.4ALPHA.tar.gz`

3. `cd ncrack-0.4ALPHA`

4. `./configure`

5. `make ; sudo make install`

You will be able to see the output of the preceding steps as shown in the
following screenshot:

```
            .$+00~?~000
            :00000.=0000
           ?00?00+=:   ,0,
     00000..0000~ 000000.     $0
     00..0~0?0::00,?0::?$0.    00 ~
   .0.    ,0?00000.0$,+,000.00 $00
   0.    00.?00=00000~0+0:000?0,~0?.
  .0  +00    0+0000 0000=?~0000?00 00
  .:  .~~   .000=00000~00=000000+0.0~0$$.
 00 ,    ?00.. 000~000000000000..:0.0:0~    0$00.+
00.0    00    00?~000~000000000+00   +  ~0000000000=$0000
   $   00   00.   .00,000000000000$.00000.    .0000+$+~00
  0   00  .0         000000000?~0000000.   0.   .0$000000+$0
 0    0   0     000:$~0000=0.0000,$.      00    0000000000
    0   00    ?.0000       $0 0 .              .0000
    .   $    ?000.                             0 0
       0    +~?000
      0.    :0000000    |=------=[ Ncrack ]=------=|
            0000$?+00
            00+0:~0$0+
            .0$000?00
             0?000000
              .000~0
Configuration complete.  Type make (or gmake on some *BSD machines) to compile.
dshaw@debian:~/ncrack-0.4ALPHA$ _
```

Upon configuration, you may notice a scorpion ASCII art (as shown in the preceding
screenshot). This art pays homage to the Nmap dragon that you may remember from
when we first installed Nmap, several chapters ago!

Once Ncrack is installed, there are several useful and interesting ways we can invoke
it to do our bidding.

```
                              2. ncrack
dshaw (warpdrive) ~ % ncrack -v ssh://localhost

Starting Ncrack 0.4ALPHA ( http://ncrack.org ) at 2015-02-13 12:41 PST
```

The most straightforward way to run Ncrack is very simple; as shown in the preceding screenshot, one may simply run `ncrack` followed by the protocol URI and hostname (or IP address) of the targeted service. Used in this way, we can attack services (such as SSH) by running `ncrack ssh://TARGET`.

Ncrack is most effective when used with a known username. For example, if we knew that a given system had a root login that allowed password authentication, we would run `ncrack --user root ssh://TARGET` to brute force against that username.

Although this functionality is very useful, it is by no means unique; many tools, such as **Hydra** and **Medusa** can run brute force attacks. The true benefits of Ncrack are revealed when Ncrack is run based on the results from an Nmap scan.

Let's say that we are conducting a penetration test or security assessment on a series of hosts across a Class C (/24) network. If, for example, 200 hosts are online—and each one has between five and ten services listening—you're looking at a lot of different brute force attempts to implement over the command line. Ncrack, however, can do this for you.

Just as Nmap can export different log types, Ncrack can read them as input—and automatically attack the services in question. For example, if we have an `-oX` flag (XML output) from an Nmap scan, Ncrack can use `-iX` to input that same list as a target file:

```
                              2. ncrack
dshaw (warpdrive) ~ % nmap scanme.nmap.org -oX scanme

Starting Nmap 6.46 ( http://nmap.org ) at 2015-02-13 13:08 PST
Nmap scan report for scanme.nmap.org (74.207.244.221)
Host is up (0.033s latency).
Not shown: 997 closed ports
PORT      STATE SERVICE
22/tcp    open  ssh
80/tcp    open  http
9929/tcp open   nping-echo

Nmap done: 1 IP address (1 host up) scanned in 0.94 seconds
dshaw (warpdrive) ~ % ncrack -iX scanme

Starting Ncrack 0.4ALPHA ( http://ncrack.org ) at 2015-02-13 13:08 PST
Service with name 'nping-echo' not supported! Ignoring...
```

We can easily see that by scanning `nmap.scanme.org` and exporting an XML file, we can easily import it to Ncrack. Although this is just one host, you can imagine how much time we would save if we used this for a large network! It's also worth noting that services that either don't support login, or that Ncrack doesn't know how to use, are by default excluded from the scan. In this case, `nping-echo` was excluded due to not having a login prompt.

There are a few flags that are absolutely necessary to run Ncrack effectively, in addition to specifying target files. The two most important flags for Ncrack are `-U` and `-P` flags, which each point to a text file containing usernames and passwords.

There are a plethora of other flags, configuration settings, and uses for Ncrack—all of which can be found on the very useful main page.

Before using Ncrack, a word of caution: while port scanning with Nmap can be irritating to many system administrators (and is, in fact, illegal in some areas), attempting to compromise a service using Ncrack is illegal and should only be done with explicit permission of the system owner. If you're trying to perform a security assessment on your own assets or if you have a signed consent form (such as in the case of a penetration test), you'll be okay—but do not attempt to compromise arbitrary hosts on the Internet!

Host detection with Nping

Much like Ncrack, Nping was added into the Nmap suite only very recently—its first iteration was created in August 2009 (along with Ncrack), and was first included in the actual Nmap suite in March 2010.

Although you might not expect it from its name, Nping does much more than ICMP echo requests (what we typically call a ping)—primarily, it can also execute ARP probes and TCP or UDP requests to given ports, in order to find out if those hosts are online based on the response. For example, if we want to debug certain network connections, we can easily use Nping to determine what's happening on the wire. The following screenshot shows a basic Nping command:

In the preceding screenshot, we ran Nping with two checks per port (-c 2, where "c" stands for "count"), and scanned ports on dshaw.net — 80. In this case, 80 is an open port (it is running my web server), and we can clearly see the responses we're expecting. As we remember from earlier chapters, we can now see exactly what is happening as the TCP handshake is attempted through network connection information (packets sent and received). If we were debugging a network connection, we would also specify -v to see even more packet information.

One of the most unique features of Nping is its built-in echo mode. The echo mode allows Nping to work as both a server and a client, and sends packets back and forth. By showing the entirety of a network connection (the packets that the client is sending, in their original state, and the packets as they are received by a server), it is extremely easy to detect network address translation, interfering intrusion prevention systems, packet shaping, and so on.

For a full list of Nping echo commands, as well as a variety of intended uses, view the Nmap documentation portal (NSEDoc), which has a comprehensive tutorial located at http://nmap.org/book/nping-man-echo-mode.html.

File transfers and backdoors with Ncat

For those who may not be familiar, a wonderful network administration tool was unveiled in 1995; it was called Netcat. This had a variety of uses, from file transfers, to network monitoring, to chat servers — even so functional as to create a backdoor — by mirroring its input to a specified network address of the user's choice. Netcat was in many ways a very lightweight port scanner — by using a quick shell script, it was extremely easy to check whether certain ports were responding on a given host.

Netcat is still in heavy use today, but the Nmap development team saw some pretty serious improvements — both in stability and usability — that they can make to the software. As such, in 2009, Ncat was released as a part of the Nmap suite.

Unlike Netcat, Ncat has SSL support (natively), great connection redirection reliability, and several other built-in features that make it a great tool in a security administrator's toolbox.

Ncat has two modes: the "listen" mode, which listens on a provided port for incoming connections, and the "connect" mode, through which commands are sent and feedback is received. In the connect mode, we can use Ncat to connect to a variety of services, including HTTP-based web servers.

Sending the `GET / HTTP/1.0` request after invoking Ncat via `ncat nmap.org 80` yields the following output:

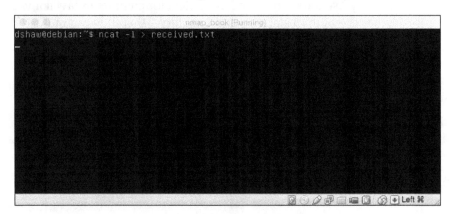

Although it clearly doesn't render as well as a web browser like Chrome or Firefox would, you can see the HTTP/HTML response from the web server quite clearly. This same functionality of Ncat can also be used to connect to many different types of services, including SMTP, FTP, POP3, and so on. When trying to send different inputs to different protocols, Ncat can be invaluable!

Ncat is also very useful when conducting a penetration test or security assessment, as it can be used as both a method for data exfiltration, and as a way to have a persistent backdoor into a compromised system.

The ability to send a file through Ncat uses both the "listen" and "connect" functionalities of the tool. The following screenshot shows a very basic Ncat command:

To begin, we set up an Ncat listener using the -1 or listen flag. Since we are expecting a file, we can pipe the output to received.txt. We always want to make sure that we are outputting the type of file that we're expecting so that we don't have to deal with changing file types at a later date. When setting up the listener, we can also set up a specific port (which is useful on penetration tests); but in this case, we left the default port of 31337 intact.

```
nmap_book [Running]
dshaw@debian:~$ cat send.txt
this is the file that we are going to send!
dshaw@debian:~$ ncat localhost < send.txt
dshaw@debian:~$ _
                                                    Left ⌘
```

We can see in the preceding screenshot that somewhere else (not in the listener) we have a file called send.txt with the this is the file that we are going to send! content. Sending the file is easy! All we need to do is invoke Ncat, point it at a localhost (again, we're using the default port of 31337 so no port specification is necessary), and pipe the input from send.txt. The following screenshot demonstrates opening a received text file:

```
nmap_book [Running]
dshaw@debian:~$ ncat -1 > received.txt
dshaw@debian:~$ cat received.txt
this is the file that we are going to send!
dshaw@debian:~$ _
                                                    Left ⌘
```

As we can see in the preceding screenshot, Ncat will automatically close out once the file is received. Once we actually receive the file, it's as simple as "cat"-ing the file we received to see that it is in fact the same content as the one we sent.

Lastly, Ncat can also be used as a backdoor, in order to create persistent access to a compromised system. The following screenshot shows this basic functionality:

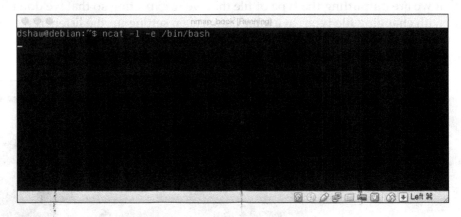

As seen in the preceding screenshot, establishing a shell connection via Ncat is very simple. We used `ncat -l -e /bin/bash` to listen on the default, and executed `/bin/bash` (our shell) when a client connected. It's worth noting that in this form, the backdoor is not persistent—meaning that it will not stay listening after the client has disconnected. The following screenshot demonstrates the ability to run Linux commands on a remote system through Ncat:

```
dshaw@debian:~$ ncat localhost
whoami
dshaw
ls
logbase.gnmap
logbase.nmap
logbase.xml
ncrack-0.4ALPHA
ncrack-0.4ALPHA.tar.gz
nmap-6.47
nmap-6.47.tar.bz2
received.txt
send.txt
```

In order to connect to the shell, as shown in the preceding screenshot, we can simply invoke `ncat localhost` (since the port is still default) and have a bash shell spawn our prompt. In this case, we ran `whoami` and received back `dshaw`, then executed a `ls` command and received a directory listing of the remote directory. While other backdoor access methods may be more reliable or complicated, it is hard to think of one more simple!

Comparing Nmap results with Ndiff

The last tool that comes packed with the Nmap suite is Ndiff. For those unfamiliar with the traditional *NIX tool "diff," it is designed to visually show the differences between two separate files of text. In other words, if you (for example) want to see which lines of code changed when a patch was applied, you can "diff" the new patch and the old code, and visually see the differences. The following screenshot shows a basic Nmap command:

```
dshaw@debian:~$ nmap -n -p80,81 dshaw.net -oX scan1.xml

Starting Nmap 6.47 ( http://nmap.org ) at 2015-02-16 17:29 PST
Nmap scan report for dshaw.net (173.255.214.88)
Host is up (0.029s latency).
PORT    STATE     SERVICE
80/tcp  open      http
81/tcp  filtered  hosts2-ns

Nmap done: 1 IP address (1 host up) scanned in 2.75 seconds
dshaw@debian:~$ _
```

In the preceding screenshot, we launched a scan against my web server—dshaw.net—for ports 80 and 81. We named our first scan `scan1.xml` and ran another scan against the same host—we called it `scan2.xml`. The only difference is that I used Ncat (which we learned about earlier in this chapter) to open up port 81 to the Internet.

In order to compare the results, we simply have to call `ndiff scan1.xml scan2.xml` — very straightforward. The following screenshot demonstrates this command:

```
dshaw@debian:~$ ndiff scan1.xml scan2.xml
-Nmap 6.47 scan initiated Mon Feb 16 17:29:39 2015 as: nmap -n -p80,81 -oX scan1
.xml dshaw.net
+Nmap 6.47 scan initiated Mon Feb 16 17:30:11 2015 as: nmap -n -p80,81 -oX scan2
.xml dshaw.net

 dshaw.net (173.255.214.88):
 PORT    STATE    SERVICE    VERSION
-81/tcp filtered hosts2-ns
+81/tcp open     hosts2-ns
dshaw@debian:~$ _
```

As you can clearly see in the preceding screenshot, the Ndiff output — which uses the same format as the traditional "diff" tool — shows + and – to indicate which lines are new or old. Since it parses through the actual XML file, rather than just the text output, Ndiff can successfully determine when new hosts were added in their entirety, rather than just being in a different place in the output. In this case, it's very clear that port 81 (with only a default "service" tag, rather than actual version scanning) was open in the second scan, but not the first. This tool is very useful for system administrators who want to view the state of their network over time.

Summary

This chapter gave an overview of the additional tools that ship with the Nmap suite, and the various tasks that we can accomplish using them. Although Nmap itself is wonderful, in order to have the full breadth of Nmap's usefulness, we need to use some of the packaged tools as well.

In the next chapter, we will learn how to use Nmap with other tools outside of the Nmap suite, in order to conduct a fully functional security assessment, or penetration tests.

9
Vulnerability Assessments and Tools

After learning all the additional tools that come packaged with the Nmap suite, it is a good idea for us to take a look at some third-party tools that can assist in conducting a vulnerability assessment. Vulnerability assessments, more than just a simple port scan, are comprehensive reports that detail the full range of vulnerabilities that may exist on a given target scope.

Some of the tools we'll learn about in this chapter interact very well with Nmap, while others are simply follow-up tools to use after the initial Nmap scan.

In this chapter, we will cover the following topics:

- Conducting a vulnerability scan with Nessus
- Assessing web server issues with Nikto
- Identifying sensitive web directories with DirBuster
- Getting started with intercepting proxies

Conducting vulnerability scans with Nessus

One of the most common pieces of software to use in conjunction with a port scanner is a vulnerability scanner. This scanner takes the role of port scanning one level higher; rather than identifying open ports and services, it cross-references these versions with a (usually proprietary) database of vulnerabilities in order to show whether a given service is vulnerable to attack.

These scanners are the key elements in vulnerability assessments, as they reduce the burden of the security engineer; instead of having to manually identify weaknesses, a scanner (that is frequently updated) can do much of that work.

Although Nessus was originally started (in 1998) as a free security scanner, it has since then been closed off to the public due to Tenable (the company Nessus' creator founded) selling the licenses instead. While many security companies pay for these licenses, you can try out a fork of the Nessus project (OpenVAS) for free.

Using Nessus is fairly straightforward. Although many security tools run on the command line (including some that we'll review later in this chapter), Nessus uses a web-based user interface that is very intuitive to use. The basic usage consists of:

- Selecting a target list (Nmap can help with this)
- Selecting a scan type
- Running the scan
- Interpreting results

The following screenshot shows the Nessus "templates" page:

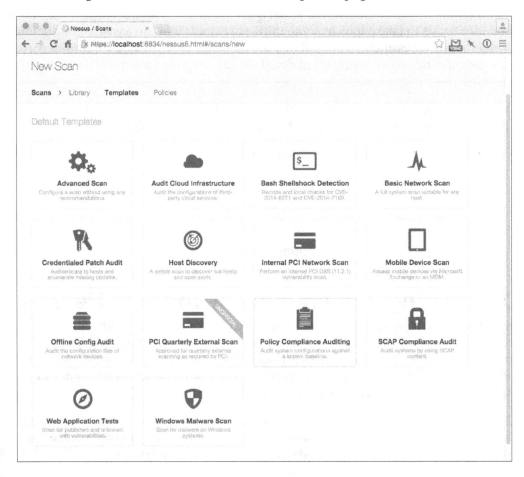

As we can see in the preceding screenshot, logging into Nessus and selecting **New Scan** allows us to choose from a variety of premade scan types—while it also allows us to select **Policies** for custom scan types. For the purpose of this scan, I have created a special scan type that will scan all ports (just like Nmap!) and then cross-reference any vulnerabilities it detects.

In order to launch the scan, we must select the targets we're looking to scan. Just like during our Nmap test scans, we'll scan scanme.nmap.org. Note that conducting a vulnerability scan on an unwilling target can be very upsetting to system administrators, and is illegal in many parts of the world:

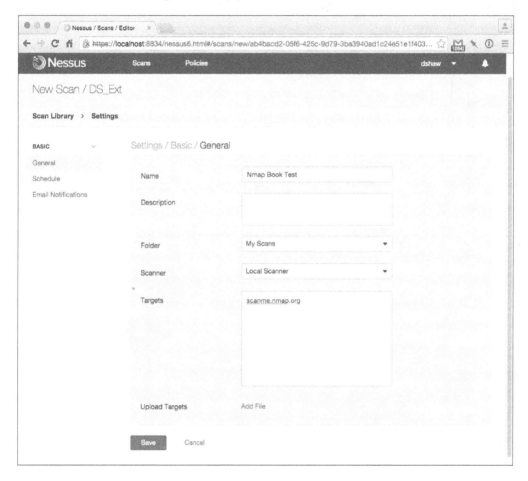

The Nessus graphical user interface is very simple to use; simply add the host to "targets," and give the scan a name. In large penetration tests, many security assessors will specifically parse out online hosts (or hosts with services listening) from the Nmap results, in order to not waste Nessus time on hosts that are either offline or do not have any services listening. The following screenshot shows a vulnerability scan in Nessus:

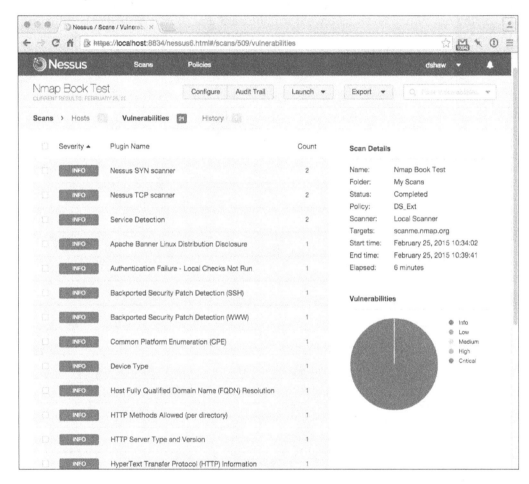

Once the scan is completed, clicking on **Vulnerabilities** shows the current list of vulnerabilities detected on the target scope. As expected, `scanme.nmap.org` has very few vulnerabilities (the Nmap team knows a lot about security!), but there are still a few "informational" findings that crop up in order to give the most information possible to the assessor. In this case, it appears that some configurations (such as the Apache web server information) allow information disclosure.

Nessus is a powerful tool, but the NSE is quickly becoming a formidable competitor — by being able to script out all of the same checks that Nessus has built-in. The advantage Nessus holds, however, is that Tenable has a full team of security engineers writing new plugins almost constantly; with Nmap scripts, someone needs to create a script, upload it to the web, and distribute it to many users before it can be used in practice.

Custom checks are another feature that Nessus can support. Much like the NSE, Nessus users may use a powerful scripting tool called the **Nessus Attack Scripting Language (NASL)**. NASL scripts can be written by anyone, and provide the full power of the Nessus engine — without necessarily running a full Nessus scan against a given host. Full NASL documentation can be accessed on the Tenable website.

Assessing web server issues with Nikto

Nikto is an open source tool that allows security assessors to evaluate the configuration of web servers. Unlike Nmap or Nessus, Nikto is designed exclusively for web-based configuration evaluations. As a general rule, it's a good idea to run Nikto (or a similar web scanner) on web services that are identified as part of a penetration test or vulnerability assessment. Nikto can be accessed from its web page at `https://cirt.net/Nikto2`.

The installation of Nikto is a fairly straightforward process, similar to the other tools we've used throughout this book:

1. `wget https://github.com/sullo/nikto/archive/master.zip`
2. `unzip master.zip`
3. `cd nikto-master/program`
4. `Nikto is now ready to use!`

Nikto, like many early security tools, is a Perl script—which means that as long as Perl is available on your system, Nikto is good to go! In order to demonstrate how Nikto works, we will run a simple scan against our favorite host, `scanme.nmap.org`. To run this scan, we invoke Nikto using the `-h` (host) flag: `nikto -h scanme.nmap.org`.

```
                                  nmap_book [Running]
+ Target IP:          74.207.244.221
+ Target Hostname:    scanme.nmap.org
+ Target Port:        80
+ Start Time:         2015-02-25 11:49:49 (GMT-8)
---------------------------------------------------------------------------
+ Server: Apache/2.2.14 (Ubuntu)
+ The anti-clickjacking X-Frame-Options header is not present.
+ The X-XSS-Protection header is not defined. This header can hint to the user a
gent to protect against some forms of XSS
+ The X-Content-Type-Options header is not set. This could allow the user agent
to render the content of the site in a different fashion to the MIME type
+ No CGI Directories found (use '-C all' to force check all possible dirs)
+ Apache/2.2.14 appears to be outdated (current is at least Apache/2.4.12). Apac
he 2.0.65 (final release) and 2.2.29 are also current.
+ Uncommon header 'tcn' found, with contents: list
+ Apache mod_negotiation is enabled with MultiViews, which allows attackers to e
asily brute force file names. See http://www.wisec.it/sectou.php?id=4698ebdc59d1
5. The following alternatives for 'index' were found: index.html
+ OSVDB-630: IIS may reveal its internal or real IP in the Location header via a
 request to the /images directory. The value is "http://127.0.0.1/images/".
+ Allowed HTTP Methods: GET, HEAD, POST, OPTIONS
+ OSVDB-3268: /icons/: Directory indexing found.
+ OSVDB-3268: /images/: Directory indexing found.
+ OSVDB-3268: /images/?pattern=/etc/*&sort=name: Directory indexing found.
                                                              Left ⌘
```

You can see in the preceding screenshot that as Nikto runs, it identifies many issues (including some of the issues we identified with Nmap and Nessus), as well as a few different configuration options—such as the lack of certain security headers, the existence of certain web directories, and so on.

In the event of actual web server vulnerabilities, Nikto can be invaluable to detect exploitable attack vectors. As time goes on, the NSE is taking more and more of these checks from Nikto and integrating them directly into Nmap—but at its core, Nmap is still a port scanner; detecting vulnerabilities is a bonus, not the primary purpose.

Identifying sensitive web directories with DirBuster

Although Nikto can identify potentially sensitive directories and web server misconfigurations, its primary purpose is not to find hidden files. DirBuster, however, exists entirely to find the hidden files and directories on web servers. Using Java (so the Java Runtime Environment must be installed), DirBuster can send many, many requests to a web server in order to completely enumerate any directories that may be interesting to any sort of an assessor. From a self-testing perspective, running DirBuster can be very useful to verify that there are no sensitive files left on your own web server!

Technically, DirBuster as a stand-alone product is considered as end of life by OWASP, the organization that runs the project. The codebase has been ported to the OWASP **Zed Attack Proxy (ZAP)** project (which we'll talk about in the next section), but DirBuster can still be run in stand-alone mode—which is very common in the information security consulting industry. You can download DirBuster at the following URL: `http://sourceforge.net/projects/dirbuster/`.

In its normal use case, DirBuster is a **Graphical User Interface (GUI)**-based software—however, the most common usage in the security industry is to use the `-H` flag, which runs DirBuster in headless mode. This mode means that the software runs on the command line, allowing easier scripting to run the software, as well as the ability to run DirBuster from "staging" servers, which are usually only accessed over SSH. Fortunately, we've become very comfortable with the command line while learning about Nmap, so this shouldn't be a problem!

Running DirBuster can be a little bit daunting for newcomers, but it's actually very simple: running `java -jar [Dirbuster file].jar -H -u http://scanme.nmap.org` will run the software against `scanme.nmap.org`. We invoke it using `java -jar` because we're running a JAR file (a packaged Java program), `-H` for headless mode (as we learned above), and `-u` before the URL of the base site we're looking to scan. Although we can scan sites with permission, DirBuster generally takes a little while to run—since it has to check many, many potential directories to give a comprehensive list. Once DirBuster is finished running or it is stopped with the "control-C" stop mechanism, a report is written to a text file in the directory DirBuster ran. This automatic log generation is very useful, since DirBuster can often find a large amount of sensitive directories.

It's interesting to note that you can specify the list that DirBuster uses to check for directories, and it's a good idea to make sure this list is always up-to-date. It's a good idea to check around the Internet for updated lists, especially as DirBuster itself is technically no longer actively maintained.

Getting started with intercepting proxies

We've now learned how to conduct full vulnerability scans using Nessus, find web server misconfigurations using Nikto, and identify sensitive files and directories using DirBuster. However, none of these tools show us how a web application may actually be communicating with a potential client browser. In order to see this level of communication, we need to use what's called an intercepting proxy.

You've probably heard of a proxy before—something you can bounce your web traffic off, in order to have a different source IP address or to avoid certain types of firewalls—but an intercepting proxy is something different altogether. While you're still bouncing your traffic somewhere else, in the case of an intercepting proxy, you're proxying to yourself and then using a piece of software to potentially modify that request.

One of the most common intercepting proxies in the security industry is Burp Suite, which has a "community" edition (free) and a "professional" edition (paid). A popular alternative to Burp Suite is OWASP ZAP, but for the purposes of demonstrating an intercepting proxy, Burp Suite does the job just fine. You can download the free edition of Burp Suite at the following URL:

```
http://portswigger.net/burp/download.html
```

The first step to set up an intercepting proxy is configuring a web browser to point at the proxy. Each proxy is different, but Burp Suite uses port 8080 as the default. This is usually in the web browser's settings, generally under the **Network** tab. Once proxying is set up, simply browsing to any page will allow the request to be intercepted.

As an example, we've set up Burp Suite to intercept requests, and attempted to use Firefox to browse to scanme.nmap.org:

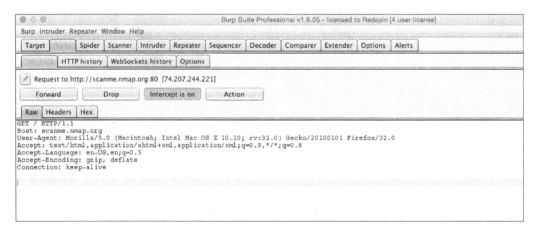

Because we have proxying to Burp Suite configured, we can immediately see that our request ("GET /") is being intercepted by Burp Suite. This is useful in and of itself, as it allows us to see exactly what our web browser is doing with the request, but there are even more functionalities to intercepting proxies. More than just seeing the requests, we can actually modify them on the wire! The following screenshot shows Burp Suite intercepting a request:

In the preceding screenshot, you can see that we changed our request from GET / to GET /TEST, which changes the request to the web server before the server receives it. Although this change is just a simple GET parameter change, this functionality is very useful when assessing web applications. For example, it can sometimes be possible to send the POST requests for other users' data by changing a variable, where simply browsing to a different URL with a web browser would not produce the intended effect. In terms of assessing web applications, an intercepting proxy is at the forefront of cutting-edge tools. The following screenshot shows a web browser interpreting the request's result:

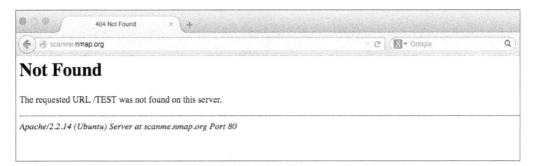

You can see that once we clicked the **Forward** button in Burp Suite, allowing the modified request to continue on to the server, our browser got a response that /TEST was not found on the server. This 404 error was produced because the request was changed on the wire, and the new file does not exist.

Burp Suite is a powerful tool, with many features—and worthy of a whole book to itself, which is also available. If you have an interest in web application security, I strongly recommend using and learning more about Burp Suite.

Summary

This chapter took us from understanding how to run port scans, to learning how other security tools fit into the security professional's daily life. We have learned how to conduct vulnerability scans and assessments with Nessus, evaluate web server configurations with Nikto, find hidden files and directories using DirBuster, and intercept and modify requests to web applications using Burp Suite.

Although there is still a lot to learn about the security world, we have now gotten to the point where conducting a vulnerability assessment is within our reach!

In the next chapter, we will learn the basics of conducting a penetration test using Metasploit, and how Nmap and Metasploit can be used in conjunction to produce an excellent attack platform.

10
Penetration Testing with Metasploit

A vulnerability assessment is only part of a full security sweep. After vulnerabilities are identified or misconfigurations are discovered, the security assessor should strive to actually exploit these vulnerabilities. The reasons for taking the assessment to the exploitation stage are numerous, but the most important parts are to eliminate false positive findings and to demonstrate the full criticality of potentially severe findings.

There is very little that will catch a Director of IT or CIO's attention faster than exfiltrating sensitive data from a supposedly secured system!

Metasploit is a very effective attack platform, with many modules being added to the system at a very quick rate. Leveraging the power of Metasploit with scanning tools such as Nmap, and vulnerability scanners such as Nessus, can complete the Trifecta of a well-prepared security tool suite.

In this chapter, we will cover the following topics:

- Installing Metasploit
- Scanning with Metasploit
- Attacking services with Metasploit
- What to learn next

Installing Metasploit

Before we can begin using Metasploit, we need to install it to our system. Unlike Nmap, installing Metasploit can be a little bit trickier — but it's nothing that a little careful work can't overcome!

The first step is to make sure that all the dependencies that Metasploit requires are installed. To do so is relatively simple, we just need to run `sudo apt-get install build-essential libreadline-dev libssl-dev libpq5 libpq-dev libreadline5 libsqlite3-dev libpcap-dev openjdk-7-jre git-core autoconf postgresql pgadmin3 curl zlib1g-dev libxml2-dev libxslt1-dev vncviewer libyaml-dev curl zlib1g-dev`:

```
                          nmap_book [Running]
 dosfstools dpkg-dev fuse gconf-service gconf2 gconf2-common git git-core
 git-man gnome-mime-data gvfs gvfs-common gvfs-daemons gvfs-libs
 krb5-multidev libaacs0 libalgorithm-diff-perl libalgorithm-diff-xs-perl
 libalgorithm-merge-perl libatasmart4 libatk-wrapper-java
 libatk-wrapper-java-jni libavahi-glib1 libbluray1 libbonobo2-0
 libbonobo2-common libcairo-gobject2 libcanberra0 libcryptsetup4 libcurl3
 libcurl3-gnutls libdconf0 libdevmapper-event1.02.1 libdpkg-perl
 liberror-perl libfam0 libfile-fcntllock-perl libgconf-2-4 libgconf2-4
 libgdu0 libgif4 libgl1-mesa-glx libglapi-mesa libglu1-mesa
 libgnome-keyring-common libgnome-keyring0 libgnome2-0 libgnome2-common
 libgnomevfs2-0 libgnomevfs2-common libgnomevfs2-extra libgssrpc4 libgtk-3-0
 libgtk-3-bin libgtk-3-common libid10 libkadm5clnt-mit8 libkadm5srv-mit8
 libkdb5-6 libkrb5-dev liblvm2app2.2 liborbit2 libparted0debian1 libpcap-dev
 libpcap0.8-dev libpq-dev libpq5 libreadline-dev libreadline6-dev librtmp0
 libsgutils2-2 libsmbclient libsqlite3-dev libssh2-1 libssl-dev libssl-doc
 libtinfo-dev libvorbisfile3 libwxbase2.8-0 libwxgtk2.8-0 libxcb-glx0
 libxcb-shape0 libxml2-dev libxslt1.1 libxslt1-dev libxv1 libxxf86dga1
 libyaml-0-2 libyaml-dev ntfs-3g openjdk-7-jre pgadmin3 pgadmin3-data pgagent
 policykit-1-gnome postgresql postgresql-9.1 postgresql-client-9.1
 postgresql-client-common postgresql-common rsync ttf-dejavu-extra udisks
 x11-utils xtightvncviewer zlib1g-dev
0 upgraded, 117 newly installed, 0 to remove and 0 not upgraded.
Need to get 56.5 MB of archives.
After this operation, 181 MB of additional disk space will be used.
Do you want to continue [Y/n]? _
```

As you can see in the preceding screenshot, most Linux machines will need to install several packages from this list that aren't included by default. Don't worry if you don't know what these individual packages do — we just need them installed so that Metasploit can function correctly.

In addition to installing various packages, we need to make sure that we have an up-to-date version of Ruby installed. Using a tool called "RVM" makes this relatively straightforward; full documentation of RVM is available at `http://rvm.io`. At the time of writing, we are installing Ruby 2.1.5 to run Metasploit:

```
hmap_book [Running]
by-2.1.5.tar.bz2
Checking requirements for debian.
Installing requirements for debian.
Updating system.....
Installing required packages: gawk, sqlite3, libgdbm-dev, libncurses5-dev, libto
ol, bison, pkg-config, libffi-dev..........
Requirements installation successful.
ruby-2.1.5 - #configure
ruby-2.1.5 - #download
  % Total    % Received % Xferd  Average Speed   Time    Time     Time  Current
                                 Dload  Upload   Total   Spent    Left  Speed
100 22.5M  100 22.5M    0     0  2975k      0  0:00:07  0:00:07 --:--:-- 5438k
No checksum for downloaded archive, recording checksum in user configuration.
ruby-2.1.5 - #validate archive
ruby-2.1.5 - #extract
ruby-2.1.5 - #validate binary
ruby-2.1.5 - #setup
ruby-2.1.5 - #gemset created /home/dshaw/.rvm/gems/ruby-2.1.5@global
ruby-2.1.5 - #importing gemset /home/dshaw/.rvm/gemsets/global.gems............-
ruby-2.1.5 - #generating global wrappers.......
ruby-2.1.5 - #gemset created /home/dshaw/.rvm/gems/ruby-2.1.5
ruby-2.1.5 - #importing gemsetfile /home/dshaw/.rvm/gemsets/default.gems evaluat
ed to empty gem list
ruby-2.1.5 - #generating default wrappers.......
dshaw@debian:~$ _
```

Once Ruby is installed, the only other requirements are Nmap (which we've already installed), configuring Postgres, and installing Metasploit itself.

Configuring Postgres is very straightforward: as `root`, simply run `su postgres` to assume that user role, and run the following two commands:

```
createuser msf -P -S -R -D
createdb -O msf msf
```

Once the Postgres database is configured, we can start working with Metasploit itself. The first step is to clone the Git repository to get the code locally, which can be achieved by running `git clone https://github.com/rapid7/metasploit-framework.git`.

Once the files have been created (in a directory called "metasploit-framework"), we can `cd` into that directory and run `bundle install`, in order to make sure Ruby gem dependencies are up-to-date. If the gems are out-of-date, `bundle update` will verify that the latest specified versions are running:

```
nmap_book [Running]
[*] Starting the Metasploit Framework console...|


                    ----------.
          .' ######## ;."
      ----,.      ;@         @@  ;     ----,..
  ."  @@@@@'.,'@@            @@@@@',.'@@@@ ".
'-.@@@@@@@@@@@@@           @@@@@@@@@@@@@ @;
  .@@@@@@@@@@@@@           @@@@@@@@@@@@@ .'
   "--'.@@@  -.@          @ `,'-  . --"
      ".@' ; @            @ `.  ;'
       |@@@@ @@@          @  .
      ' @@@ @@           @@         ,
      .@@@@ @@          @@         .
      ',@@      @      ;
       ( 3 C    )       /|___ / Metasploit! \
      ;@'. __*__,."    \|--- _____/
       '(.,...."/


     =[ metasploit v4.11.0-dev [core:4.11.0.pre.dev api:1.0.0]]
+ -- --=[ 1412 exploits - 800 auxiliary - 229 post      ]
+ -- --=[ 361 payloads - 37 encoders - 8 nops           ]
+ -- --=[ Free Metasploit Pro trial: http://r-7.co/trymsp ]

msf > _
```

At this stage, Metasploit is installed! We have no need to compile anything, since Metasploit is written in Ruby (which is an interpreted language, rather than a compiled one). To start Metasploit, simply run `./msfconsole` while in the metasploit-framework directory—and that's all it takes!

Scanning with Metasploit

While Nmap's primary strength lies in performing fast, scalable port scans, and Nessus's forte is conducting in-depth vulnerability scans and misconfiguration detection checks, Metasploit excels in actually exploiting vulnerabilities on a one-off basis. In a security assessment, Metasploit is generally brought to the table as a last step: once the vulnerabilities are enumerated from other tools, Metasploit can actually exploit them. Sensitive data, compromised machines, and more, can easily be exfiltrated using Metasploit and a variety of tools that come packaged with the framework.

Metasploit can easily have a whole book dedicated to its usage—and, in fact, it does—but we'll go over the basic scanning and exploitation techniques so that you can implement it into your everyday processes, without too much of a hassle.

The easiest way to launch a scan for a particular vulnerability (or information gathering technique) is simply to use it. The way to specify a use command is simply run use primary/secondary/module in Metasploit. The following screenshot shows us setting up an HTTP version scan in Metasploit:

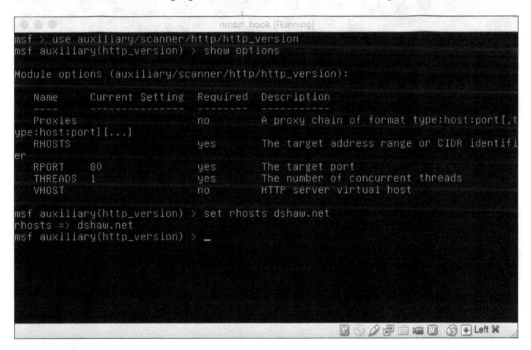

As you can easily see in the preceding screenshot, we've decided to use the
`auxiliary/scanner/http/http_version` module to check HTTP versions.
Once we have the module selected, we check what options are available by running
"show options." In this case, we need to specify that `rhosts` should be our target web
server. Because this is plural (hosts, not 'host'), you can tell that we can theoretically
scan an Internet range from this directive. A brief description is also written in
the **Description** tab of this window. The following screenshot shows options for a
Metasploit scan:

```
                                    nmap_book [Running]
msf > use auxiliary/scanner/http/http_version
msf auxiliary(http_version) > show options

Module options (auxiliary/scanner/http/http_version):

   Name         Current Setting  Required  Description
   ----         ---------------  --------  -----------
   Proxies                       no        A proxy chain of format type:host:port[,t
ype:host:port] [...]
   RHOSTS                        yes       The target address range or CIDR identifi
er
   RPORT        80               yes       The target port
   THREADS      1                yes       The number of concurrent threads
   VHOST                         no        HTTP server virtual host

msf auxiliary(http_version) > set rhosts dshaw.net
rhosts => dshaw.net
msf auxiliary(http_version) > run

[*]  173.255.214.88:80 nginx
[*]  Scanned 1 of 1 hosts (100% complete)
[*]  Auxiliary module execution completed
msf auxiliary(http_version) > _
```

The preceding screenshot illustrates that running the module is simple — done just
by invoking the `run` command — and we get the results we're looking for! In this
case, we receive `nginx` as the version for my web server.

It's worth noting that there are many auxiliary modules, especially "scanners"
for various different vulnerabilities and exploits. You don't always have to
actually attack a service in order to find out whether it's vulnerable!

Attacking services with Metasploit

As we learned earlier in this chapter, Metasploit's claim to fame is as an attack platform. Every day, Metasploit modules are being written and submitted to the Metasploit project; each of which can either perform a scan or, more often, actually attack a given vulnerability.

Metasploit's ability to act as an attack was revolutionary when it first debuted: rather than searching for proofs of concepts — or writing their own, after a vulnerability was announced — security professionals were immediately able to use a reliable platform with vetted modules to launch their attacks. Metasploit is written in Ruby, so it's portable to almost any platform — and since all the modules run on the framework, there is no reason to hope a proof of concept will run on whatever type of machine the user happens to currently be using.

The first step to launch a successful attack is using the "search" feature of Metasploit to look for a given module. There are a lot of ways you can use the search functionality, but for our purposes, we're just going to look for something relatively straightforward: MS08-067, a well-known vulnerability in Windows that can give us quite a lot of access if we use it correctly!

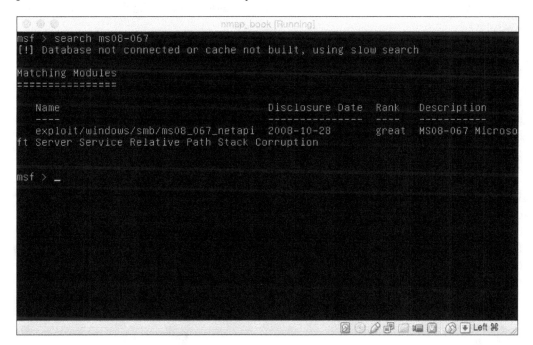

We can select the module by invoking `use`, and then set the options we need by listing them out with `show options`. It's worth noting in the preceding screenshot that each Metasploit module can have a rank—in our case, the matching module came back "great." Great! Lastly, you might notice that the initial response from Metasploit is that we don't have a database connected, so we're using `slow search`. While it's true that connecting the Postgres database that we made earlier to Metasploit would make a lot of sense, it's not always the fastest way to proceed if we're just looking to run a quick exploit.

After setting our target with `rhost`, we can run the exploit by typing `exploit`. Note that this is different than simply running a scan—Metasploit wants to ensure that you're well aware that you're launching an exploit.

When the exploit is successfully run, you will open a `meterpreter` session. You can always view open sessions by running the `sessions` command.

Meterpreter is a powerful tool that lives in the memory of a compromised machine. From Meterpreter, it is possible to run a large variety of commands—including attacks from Metasploit itself—in order to exfiltrate data to another system, or to pivot further into a compromised network. A chain of Meterpreter shells can easily compromise an entire network, and exfiltrate all sensitive data back to the source of the attacks—in this case, us!

What to learn next

Like a security program itself, learning about information security is always a process—never a finished state. Although we have learned the basics of networking; how to become a power user of Nmap (and the other tools in the Nmap suite); how to conduct a vulnerability scan; and, now, how to conduct a penetration test—there are millions of other topics available to pursue.

While there's no set curriculum to become a security professional or to continue one's education in the field, there are many more books on the subject—and many different topics to cover. I strongly recommend you to look into *The Web Application Hacker's Handbook*, if web application assessments is interesting to you. There are also countless books on Metasploit, Burp Suite Professional, exploit development, reverse engineering, malware analysis, and many more topics that you can explore.

Never stop learning!

Summary

In this chapter, we learned how to install Metasploit, conduct scans for specific vulnerabilities or information leaks using Metasploit, and actually exploit these vulnerabilities in order to conduct a successful attack. From there, we learned about Meterpreter, including how to view sessions and the ability to pivot further into a target network.

Metasploit is a powerful framework used to exploit network-based vulnerabilities, and it deserves a front-row seat to any security assessment.

Thank you for taking the time to read this book. While we have made every effort to keep the information in this book as up-to-date as possible, the security world — especially the world of security tools — is always changing. Please feel free to reach out to me for updated information, should it become necessary. Happy hacking!

Index

Symbol

.gnmap file 20

A

Amazon Web Services (AWS) 16

B

backdoor
  Ncat, using as 70, 71
bleeding edge 3
Burp Suite
  URL 80

C

categories, Nmap scripts
  auth 47
  broadcast 47
  brute 47
  default 47
  Denial of Service (DoS) 47
  discovery 47
  exploit 47
  external 47
  fuzzer 47
  intrusive 47
  malware 47
  safe 47
  version 47
  vuln 47
customized host group sizes 38

D

default scan
  running 17
DirBuster
  about 79
  sensitive web directories,
      identifying with 79
  URL 79

F

file transfers
  performing, Ncat used 67-69
FIN scan 30

G

grep-able nmap output 20

H

host detection
  Nping used 66, 67
  methods 25, 26
Hydra 65
Hypertext Transfer Protocol (HTTP) 57

I

information security 90
intercepting proxies
  defining 80-82
Intrusion Detection Systems (IDS) 30

ping agnostic scan
  running 27
port scanning 10
Postgres
  configuring 85
probe rates
  delaying 41, 42
  increasing 41, 42

R

reason flag
  defining 21, 22
RVM
  URL 85

S

scans
  logging 19-21
sensitive web directories
  identifying, with DirBuster 79
service banners 11, 12
services
  attacking, Metasploit used 89, 90
  attacking, Ncrack used 63-66
service version scan
  running 18, 19
shortport 57
specified scan ranges
  defining 21
structure, Internet 7, 8
stuck hosts
  dealing with 39-41
SYN/ACK response 22
SYN request 22

T

target
  selecting 15, 16
TCP 10
tcpdump 33
TCP scans 29, 30
TCP three-way handshake 11
traceroute 33

U

UDP services
  about 10
  scanning 28, 29

V

verbosity, in scans
  increasing 32, 33
Virtual Private Server (VPS) 16
Voice over IP (VoIP) 11
vulnerability scans
  conducting, Nessus used 73-77

W

web server issues
  assessing, Nikto used 77, 78

X

Xmas Tree scan 30

Z

Zed Attack Proxy (ZAP) 79
zero packet reconnaissance 28

Thank you for buying
Nmap Essentials

About Packt Publishing

Packt, pronounced 'packed', published its first book, *Mastering phpMyAdmin for Effective MySQL Management*, in April 2004, and subsequently continued to specialize in publishing highly focused books on specific technologies and solutions.

Our books and publications share the experiences of your fellow IT professionals in adapting and customizing today's systems, applications, and frameworks. Our solution-based books give you the knowledge and power to customize the software and technologies you're using to get the job done. Packt books are more specific and less general than the IT books you have seen in the past. Our unique business model allows us to bring you more focused information, giving you more of what you need to know, and less of what you don't.

Packt is a modern yet unique publishing company that focuses on producing quality, cutting-edge books for communities of developers, administrators, and newbies alike. For more information, please visit our website at www.packtpub.com.

About Packt Open Source

In 2010, Packt launched two new brands, Packt Open Source and Packt Enterprise, in order to continue its focus on specialization. This book is part of the Packt Open Source brand, home to books published on software built around open source licenses, and offering information to anybody from advanced developers to budding web designers. The Open Source brand also runs Packt's Open Source Royalty Scheme, by which Packt gives a royalty to each open source project about whose software a book is sold.

Writing for Packt

We welcome all inquiries from people who are interested in authoring. Book proposals should be sent to author@packtpub.com. If your book idea is still at an early stage and you would like to discuss it first before writing a formal book proposal, then please contact us; one of our commissioning editors will get in touch with you.

We're not just looking for published authors; if you have strong technical skills but no writing experience, our experienced editors can help you develop a writing career, or simply get some additional reward for your expertise.

Nmap 6: Network Exploration and Security Auditing Cookbook

ISBN: 978-1-84951-748-5   Paperback: 318 pages

A complete guide to mastering Nmap 6 and its scripting engine, covering practical tasks for penetration testers and system administrators

1. Master the power of Nmap 6.

2. Learn how the Nmap Scripting Engine works and develop your own scripts!.

3. 100% practical tasks, relevant and explained step-by-step with exact commands and optional arguments description.

Penetration Testing with Perl

ISBN: 978-1-78328-345-3   Paperback: 332 pages

Harness the power of Perl to perform professional penetration testing

1. Write your own custom information security tools using Perl and object-oriented Perl modules.

2. Apply powerful Perl Regular Expression syntax to finely tune intelligence gathering techniques.

3. Develop a clear understanding of how common attacking tools can function during a penetration test.

Please check **www.PacktPub.com** for information on our titles

PACKT open source
community experience distilled

Building Virtual Pentesting Labs
for Advanced Penetration Testing

Building Virtual Pentesting Labs for Advanced Penetration Testing

ISBN: 978-1-78328-477-1   Paperback: 430 pages

Build intricate virtual architecture to practice any penetration testing technique virtually

1. Build and enhance your existing pentesting methods and skills.

2. Get a solid methodology and approach to testing.

3. Step-by-step tutorial helping you build complex virtual architecture.

Expert Metasploit
Penetration Testing
Abhinav Singh

Expert Metasploit Penetration Testing [Video]

ISBN: 978-1-78216-366-4   Duration: 01:53 hours

Enhance your knowledge of penetration testing using Metasploit

1. Step-by-step demonstration of the Metasploit framework using real-time examples, diagrams, and presentations for theoretical topics.

2. Includes a detailed understanding of the framework internals and how they work.

3. Covers all three phases of penetration testing in detail including additional tools, such as Armitage, Nmap, and Nessus.

Please check **www.PacktPub.com** for information on our titles